THE AGAINST NATURE
Issue #1 Su.

Collection Missions-Étrangères.

Martyre des Bienheureux MI, DUONG, et TRUAT, Catéchistes annamites,
étranglés au Tonkin, le 18 Octobre 1838.

THE AGAINST NATURE JOURNAL
Issue #1 Summer 2020

EDITORS
Aimar Arriola, Grégory Castéra

CONTRIBUTING EDITOR
Giulia Tognon

COPY EDITOR
Laura Preston

PROOFREADER
Sriwhana Spong

EDITORIAL COMMITTEE
Aimar Arriola, Thomas Boutoux, Grégory Castéra,
Arvind Narrain, Sandra Terdjman, Giulia Tognon

ADVISORY COMMITTEE
Nikita Dhawan, Taru Elfving, Karim Nammour,
Piergiorgio Pepe, Graeme Reid, Nizar Saghieh

COMMUNICATION
Abi Tariq

ASSISTANT
Yundi Wang

DESIGNER
Julie Peeters

COVER ART
Stepan Lipatov

PUBLISHER
Council
info@council.art   www.council.art

ADVERTISING
Giulia Tognon
advertising@againstnaturejournal.com

DIRECTORS, COUNCIL
Grégory Castéra, Sandra Terdjman

COUNCIL BOARD
Haro Cumbusyan, Sofía Hernández Chong Cuy, Joana Hadjithomas,
Bruno Latour, Laurent Le Bon, Joseph Lemarchand,
Piergiorgio Pepe, Valérie Pihet

www.theagainstnaturejournal.com
Instagram: @theagainstnaturejournal

T.A.N.J.

The Against Nature Journal is a biannual arts and human rights magazine exploring "crime against nature" laws and their legacies, in print, in person, and online.

T.A.N.J. is published in summer and winter every year at 41 boulevard de Strasbourg, 75010, Paris.

500 copies are distributed in selected bookshops worldwide. €15 / £13 / $16 per issue

1,500 free copies are distributed internationally to individuals and organizations who are concerned with the laws of "crime against nature" and operate in the fields of law, activism, social sciences, and the arts. To join this network, please write to: distribution@theagainstnaturejournal.com

Help maintain the publishing, education, and community activities of *The Against Nature Journal* by joining our membership program. Annual membership from €45 / £40 / $50. As a French non-for-profit Association Loi 1901, Council welcomes support at all levels of giving and all gifts are tax-deductible to the full extent of the law. For further information, please write to: gregory@theagainstnaturejournal.com

Future issues will intertwine six themes, each becoming the major focus of one issue: Religion, Migration, Medicine, Love, Death, Nature. If you would like to contribute or send us a letter, please write to: editors@theagainstnaturejournal.com

Copyright © 2020 Council. All rights reserved under international and French authorship conventions. No part of this publication may be reproduced in any form without written permission from the publisher.

Issue #1 published in July 2020
Legal deposit in September 2020

ISSN 978-2-492073-00-7

Printed in Germany by Benedict Press in an edition of 2,000 copies
Paper: Munken Print Cream by Arctic Paper

Significant support for *The Against Nature Journal* is provided by the Foundation for Arts Initiatives, Kone Foundation, and Nordic Culture Point.

Dayna Ash

is a cultural and social activist, playwright, performance poet, and the founder and executive director of the nonprofit arts organization Haven for Artists, based in Beirut, Lebanon.

Naoufal Bouzid

is an African LGBTI activist from Morocco. He is the cofounder of Equality Morocco. For over ten years he has worked with local and international human rights NGOs and been involved in different campaigns for the decriminalization of homosexuality and raising awareness of LGBTI issues in Morocco.

Chekwube Danladi

is the winner of the 2019 Cave Canem Poetry Prize for her manuscript *Semiotics*, soon to be published by University of Georgia Press (September 2020). From Lagos by way of West Baltimore, she currently lives in Chicago.

Lorraine Daston

is director of the Max Planck Institute for the History of Science in Berlin and a visiting professor at the Committee on Social Thought, University of Chicago. She is the coauthor of *Wonders and the Order of Nature, 1150–1750* (with Katherine Park, Zone Books, 1998) and *Objectivity* (with Peter Galison, Zone Books, 2007).

Pawan Dhall

has been engaged with queer activism in India since the 1990s. He runs Varta Trust, Kolkata, a nonprofit for gender and sexuality issues. He researches and writes on the histories, health, and socioeconomic inclusion concerns of queer communities. His most recent publication is *Out of Line and Offline: Queer Mobilizations in '90s Eastern India* (Seagull Books, 2020).

Vivek Divan

is a queer activist and a qualified lawyer, having worked on queer rights, health, and law for over two decades, including playing a central role in the litigation challenging Section 377 of the Indian Penal Code. He heads the Centre for Health Equity, Law and Policy, in Pune, India.

Amatesiro Dore

is currently an ICORN, Region of Tuscany fellow living in Florence. He graduated from the Farafina Trust Creative Writing Workshop in 2009. In 2019, he was a writer in residence of the Wole Soyinka Foundation.

Eliel Jones

is a (queer) critic, writer, and associate curator at Cell Project Space, London. He has written about contemporary art and performance for *Artforum, Elephant, Flash Art, Frieze, The Guardian, MAP, Mousse*, and elsewhere.

Kari Mugo

is a Kenyan creative writer, activist, and a regular contributor to various online media outlets where she covers entertainment, culture, global mobility, politics, and travel. Her work has also appeared on radio, podcasts, and on stage and discusses feminism, immigration, and queer identity.

Martti Nissinen

is a Finnish theologian and professor of Old Testament Studies, University of Helsinki. He is an expert on the prophetic phenomenon in the ancient Eastern Mediterranean, but his research interests also include love poetry, homoeroticism, and masculinity.

Niza

is a feminist journalist and activist from Kuala Lumpur, Malaysia. She graduated with a degree in journalism in 2011 and has twelve years of work experience in matters of civil society.

Abu Nuwas

(Abū Nuwās al-Ḥasan ibn Hānî al-Ḥakam) is commonly regarded as one of the greatest classical Arabic poets. Living in the late eighth century, Nuwas relished wine and carnal (often same-sex) relations, both of which he refers to in his poetry.

Donnya Piggott

has been an LGBTQ advocate for almost ten years, a columnist, an award-winning social entrepreneur, and the founder of Pink Coconuts, a tech platform for LGBTQ people across the Caribbean.

Achal Prabhala

is a researcher and writer living in Bangalore. He works on providing access to medicine in India, Brazil, and South Africa. He also writes for a variety of small magazines around the world.

Linn Marie Tonstad

teaches Christian theology and gender and sexuality studies at Yale Divinity School. She is the author of two books: *God and Difference: The Trinity, Sexuality, and the Transformation of Finitude* (Routledge, 2016) and *Queer Theology: Beyond Apologetics* (Cascade Books, 2018).

Viviane Vergueiro

is a researcher and transfeminist activist working from Salvador, Bahia, Brazil. A PhD candidate in Gender Studies at Universidade Federal da Bahia, she is also part of the research center Núcleo de pesquisa e extensão em Culturas, Gêneros e Sexualidades at the university, and a project coordinator for Akahatá, a team working to advance LGBT and sexual rights.

Binyavanga Wainaina

was a Kenyan author, journalist, and the 2002 winner of the Caine Prize for African Writing. In 2014, *Time* magazine included him in their annual list of "100 Most Influential People" in the world.

Sexual and gender identities are varied and contextual: cultures and struggles and the degree of intersectionality change from one context to another. This is expressed in the use of a variety of acronyms and initialisms, from the most common LGBT to the more recent LGBTQI+, all intended to emphasize the diverse culture of sexuality and gender identities. Throughout this journal the editors have chosen to maintain each author's initialism of choice to reflect the diversity of positions.

LETTERS

Letters of response, commentary, hopes, and suggestions. This issue features some of our very first collaborators, long before the project became printed matter. If you would like to send us a letter, please write to editors@theagainstnaturejournal.com

I participated in the *Manufacturing of Rights* workshop in Beirut in 2014–15. It was inspiring to think and work with multidisciplinary artists and scholars and curators on our shared interests in the idea of "nature" and how it is constructed through legal, archival, discursive, aesthetic, and aural practices. The announcement of the "natural" is the simultaneous inauguration of the "unnatural" and vice versa. Filmmaker Carlos Motta and I collaborated on a screenplay for the workshop, and Council and Ashkal Alwan coproduced the film which became *Deseos /Raghbat.*

 The power of declaring or assuming that something is natural (heterosexuality, a binary gender system) is amplified through association with nature (something that is just there, like a mountain or a river). This association perhaps betrays more than it reveals, as human beings are currently in the process of killing and replacing this thing we call "nature." Meanwhile, the discursive power of the natural—whether it be deployed to describe sexualities, genders, racial capitalism, or the intersectional precarity of pandemics—continues to be amplified.

 Today, writing from the home I rarely leave, the idea of an in-person workshop has the feeling of risk, unfamiliarity, and even a sense of the unnatural. Did we really hug and kiss each other goodbye every day? Did we really share cigarettes and crowd into loud rooms and hotly whisper deep thoughts so close, literally into each other's naked faces? The pandemic has modulated the natural and the unnatural and stressed the affective registers of its binary relation. Viruses are not the only things that incubate in groups, so does creativity, debate, inspiration, desire, and fear.

 I miss incubating with my comrades at *Manufacturing of Rights*, and I wonder what we might come up with, how we might feel the natural and the unnatural together, today.

Maya Mikdashi
 Professor Gender Studies /Middle East Studies,
 Rutgers University

It is with great anticipation that I await the first issue of *The Against Nature Journal* on the theme of religion. I was drawn to this project through my work at Human Rights Watch. The prohibition of "carnal knowledge against the order of nature" echoes down the centuries, with legal consequences to this day. Last year, for example, a Zambian couple was sentenced to fifteen years behind bars for crimes "against nature."

When codifying English law, the seventeenth-century jurist Sir Edward Coke defined "buggery" as "a detestable, and abominable sin, amongst Christians not to be named, committed by carnal knowledge against the ordinance of the Creator, and order of nature." In the terrain of sexual morality, what is deemed "natural" is invariably a subjective interpretation of the moral order, where "natural" is conflated with religious morality and codified in law.

In the past decade, there has been a promising overall trend toward decriminalization, as colonial-era statutes have been successfully challenged in courts or revised by lawmakers. But some countries, including Gabon and Chad, have moved in the opposite direction. Brunei even legislated the death penalty for consensual sex between men in 2019, purportedly in the name of religion.

The idea that a sexual act between consenting adults can be regarded as "unnatural" and hence a threat to family, society, and the nation is a curious one and a powerful one used to mobilize against the human rights of sexual and gender minorities. *The Against Nature Journal* arrives at a timely moment, amid remarkable progress and considerable challenges. I am proud and honored to be associated with this important intervention.

Graeme Reid
   Director, LGBT Rights Program,
   Human Rights Watch

Back in 2015, we worked with some of *The Against Nature Journal* team on an ambitious project tackling contra naturam legislation across the world and the impact colonization had on establishing such legislation in so many countries, especially in the Global South, which ultimately resulted in the prosecution and criminalization of LGBTQI persons in these societies. The project adopted a multidisciplinary approach, gathering jurists, social science researchers, and artists from all over the world and aimed to deconstruct contra naturam laws as another form of decolonization.

In Lebanon, such legislation is embodied in Article 534 of the Penal Code, which criminalizes any "carnal conjunction against the order of nature." That article has been used historically to prosecute and criminalize LGBTQI persons in the country, thus exacerbating their marginalization and already vulnerable status in society. Our work in the last fifteen years has successfully deconstructed the article before national courts by adopting a strategic approach of litigation as a form of advocacy to defend persons being prosecuted on that basis, eventually affecting national jurisprudence and the contra naturam concept itself from a legal point of view.

We eagerly await *The Against Nature Journal* and expect it to generate a successful counterdiscourse on the contra naturam notion within a decolonization perspective.

Nizar Saghieh
Lawyer, activist, and co-founder,
Legal Agenda

Karim Nammour
Lawyer, activist, and board member,
Legal Agenda

I am excited to finally see the first issue of *The Against Nature Journal*. I'm very interested in this project because as one of the lawyers who were part of contesting Section 377 in India, I have always been conscious of the fact that challenging the "laws against nature" did not only mean getting rid of the archaic Section 377 of the Indian Penal Code but also questioning the social morality which these laws encoded. The challenge to the law had to become a challenge to societal prejudice itself. To challenge encrusted ways of thinking and acting that limit the freedom and dignity of LGBTQI persons, one needs to also work in the domain of activism and art. It is in this context that *The Against Nature Journal* has an important role to play in questioning the prejudicial moralities which stunt LGBTQI lives.

Arvind Narrain
Lawyer and Director of Research and Practice,
ARC International

Thinking through Religion

The inaugural issue of *The Against Nature Journal* delves into the complex and sometimes contradictory ways in which sexual and gender minorities are considered and shaped by world religions, including Christianity, Islam, Hinduism, and their denominations. The concept of "against nature" as a kind of dividing machine between what is natural and what is deviant is rooted in religious morality. The conceptual framework of our project is situated as an active response to the so-called laws against nature that still criminalize sexual and gender minorities in many parts of the world. We recognize that for various belief systems "nature" is the expression of the divine, a superior force that is separate from yet threatened by human action. It is common in most religious traditions to conform to God's judgment of whether a body or an act is either natural or unnatural. Religion as well as spirituality more generally are also sites from which to imagine and live a different relationship to the divine.

This first issue points to the historical foundations of determining the "unnatural" within dominant belief systems. Khanu vs Emperor (1925) is a case in point: one of the most influential lawsuits in Indian anti-sodomy law, it redefined the scope of Section 377, and for many years became the guiding judgment for interpreting anti-sodomy laws throughout the British colonies of South Asia, East Asia, and East Africa, as lawyer and activist Vivek Divan reflects on. How anti-sodomy laws in these regions play out today is evident in the Columns section of this journal, focused on current news from such places where against nature laws still prevail (including India, Lebanon, Malaysia, Morocco, Kenya, and the Caribbean), along with debates from Europe, Latin America, and Brazil, where there are continual regressions of reproductive, sexual orientation, and gender identity rights.

While often perceived as repressive and constraining, religion and even less regulated faiths and forms of spirituality have been and continue to be the refuge in which artists, writers, poets, and activists rethink the question of what is "natural." A special focus of this issue is on the literary practice and activism of Kenyan, gay, HIV-positive writer Binyavanga Wainaina (or the Binj, as he was so fondly called), who passed away in May 2019. Described by the *New York Times* as a "pioneering voice in African literature," Wainaina not only inspired a new generation of writers in Africa but his work served to critique the spread of homophobia by Pentecostalism and the politicization of homosexuality. And yet, Wainaina also embarked on a personal spiritual quest. Writer Amatesiro Dore, one of many protégés mentored by Wainaina at the Farafina Trust Creative Writing Workshop in Nigeria, pays tribute to his lifework in these pages alongside the first piece of fiction that Wainaina ever wrote (originally published in 1996 on a now defunct literary website, but made available in print here for the first time). This early story is, somewhat surprisingly, about pagan spirituality and is accompanied by an introduction written by Achal Prabhala. Dore's own breakthrough poem "Joy," a beautiful, queer take on sexuality and religion, has also been republished as another companion piece.

The issue showcases progressive approaches to religious thinking and practice that contribute to the ways in which we experience our own "nature," our own sexual and gender identities. Theologians Martti Nissinen and Linn Marie Tonstad, coming from differing perspectives, provide inspirational reflections on this matter. Nissinen's text, originally published in 1998, reviews the "unnatural" as intrinsic to ideas of creation and gender in the biblical world. Tonstad, in a text specially commissioned for this issue, questions from a queer perspective who the "we" implicated by the journal might be. These essays are accompanied by the poetry of Abu Nuwas, one of the most important poets of the Islamic world in the eighth century, and contemporary, queer writer Chekwube Danladi. They both welcome an accommodating spirituality.

Danh Vo inaugurates the artist contributions of *The Against Nature Journal*. Vo's conceptual art practice is concerned with the histories and meanings of sacred objects across cultures. He shares two bodies of work on this issue's theme, both of which consider the intertwinement of religion, colonialism, sexuality, and ultimately violence. Originally documentation, these reworked testimonies of Catholic missionaries in the nineteenth century and the personal records of the sexual behavior of American agents in Vietnam show Vo's long-term commitment to finding poetic spaces and elegant forms for objects that carry contradictions and speak to power.

The closing section of the journal is dedicated to the central topic of "against nature" and the related terms of "natural order" and "nature" itself. Across all editions, this section will be dedicated to key theoretical texts, making accessible to our readers a potential resource for advocacy. This issue includes the writing of Lorraine Daston, whose far-reaching philosophical work on our guiding concept has been an inspiration since the beginning of the project. Her essay is accompanied by a world chart illustrating the geographic scope of the against nature laws.

All in all, the contributions to this inaugural issue of *The Against Nature Journal*, which can be read in order, out of order, altogether, or as individual reflections, expand our understanding of nature, religion, and social justice in important and exciting ways.

Aimar Arriola
Editor

TOWARD A MORE INCLUSIVE SPIRITUALITY

ARTIST CONTRIBUTION
Danh Vo

COLUMNS

A glimpse into LGBTQI+ life and culture, struggles and hopes from across the world. Featuring regular contributions by activists, writers, and scholars from places where against nature laws still prevail and where there are continual regressions of reproductive, sexual orientation, and gender identity rights.

Pride in Jesus Church Service: Bridging the Divide in Barbados and the Caribbean

Donnya Piggott

It is no secret that religion largely fuels the rampant homophobia that exists in the world. More specifically, it fuels the homophobia that exists in the Caribbean where I live and where I tirelessly pursue with others a path toward equality and justice for all people.

It then raises the question as to why Barbados–Gays, Lesbians and All-Sexualities against Discrimination (B-GLAD), the organization which I've led for seven years, would host a Pride in Jesus church service during Pride Month in 2019.

Much like other LGBTQ organizations across the Caribbean region, our main adversary has always been the Christian church. They argue that homosexuality equates to a demonic spirit, as preached at rallies across the island, or is against the natural order of man, or further that it is "the erosion of the fabric of society."

Despite some pushback from within the church itself, the resistance to such beliefs in the local LGBTQ community has created much discussion. The church is still a source of trauma for LGBTQ people—many of whom left the church quite some years ago. Feelings of rejection, self-hate, and inadequacy stem from our early experiences with religion. So, the question remains: Why would we host such an event?

A church service with song, prayer, and worship allows believers in the Christian faith to have important conversations about equality. Barbados is touted as a Christian nation. Yet, over the years the church has only demonstrated fear, spread misinformation, and blocked the progress of the LGBTQ community. Our church service was an effort to heal and overcome that divide. This is where real progress is made, by building bridges.

Christians who believe in equality, fairness, justice, and love exist, of course: they are often the ones who send us encouraging notes to our in-boxes or quietly stop us in the street. They recognize that the LGBTQ community needs to be protected and not denounced. There are also Christian–LGBTQ people, who in existing within this intersection more often hide their own sexualities but support us from the shadows. We accept them for living their truths, too. It's important that they are not forgotten.

As expected, the event caused quite a stir. Leading antigay religious leaders attended, quietly listened, and discussed among themselves, sometimes disagreeing with the need and relevance of such an event and interrupting with opinions. However, the service allowed all religious leaders, falling either side of the LGBTQ inclusion argument, to hear each other out and

share in common scripture, dif-
fering experiences, and various
perspectives.

If we are going to embrace and
celebrate diversity, we must be
inclusive. As a non-Christian mem-
ber of the LGBTQ community, I may
not know the direct outcome of the
dialogue for Christian people. But I
do believe that it was a step in the
right direction because real change
starts with just that—dialogue.

Antigender Agendas as Colonial Reestablishments in Brazil and Abya Yala

Viviane Vergueiro

Two episodes from the Brazilian con-
text that occurred in the last year
might be useful for reflecting
on antigender agendas in our
regional political contexts. The first,
a legislative attempt in the state of
São Paulo to establish "biological
sex as the only criterion for the
definition of competitors' gender"
in professional sports (Assembleia
Legislativa, no. 346, April 2, 2019);
the other, violent remarks made
by Jair Bolsonaro, (still) the coun-
try's president, about a Rede Globo
TV program on trans women and
travestis in prison, after the cause
of imprisonment of one interviewee
was publicized.

By bringing these incidents
together, I invite consideration on
the connections between antigender
agendas (as proposed by Sexuality
Policy Watch) and the idea of "colo-
nial reestablishment." I consider
this as a theoretical assemblage of
bio-necropolitics and colonialities
(of power, knowledge, being) that
constitute socioeconomic *disposi-
tifs* and force multipliers, which
legitimize, actualize, and normal-
ize the past, present, and future
of sociocultural and geopolitical
relationships. Colonial reestablish-
ment is a present political desire
for many worldwide: a "natural"
order of things based on supremacist
perspectives and hierarchies placed
between existences. In this sense,
the two episodes are illustrations of
institutional exclusion and offenses,
perpetrated by political represen-
tatives against trans and gender
nonconforming peoples, and both
evoke a space-time that amounts to
at least five hundred years of white,
European genocide.

The connections between these
events also situate the complexity
around the perspectives and rights
regarding gender identities, gender
expressions, and sex characteristics
in resisting against antigender agen-
das. As detailed in the "Rights at
Risk" report by the Observatory on
the Universality of Rights in 2017,
it is important to realize how such
agendas are promoted and funded
by secular and religious stakehold-
ers at various levels, and how they
affect various groups through dif-
ferent strategies. As some countries
implement sex/gender-based social

segregation measures during the Covid-19 pandemic, it seems important to map the elements that drive societies' imaginaries.

These interconnections bring forth the worldwide precarization of socioeconomic rights and autonomy, particularly of marginalized groups, including LGBTI people, in the intersections of race and class. They also highlight the need to locate sociohistorical specificities in understanding the ways in which power operates within colonial ideologies, industrial revolutions, and supremacist projects.

When a bill excluding trans women from professional sports is proposed—ignoring directions from international bodies on the issue—it is not a mere act of excluding a social group from an occupation. A deeper question arises: Can trans politics allow us to better regard broader economic injustices of gendered bio-necropolitics? Could it contribute to a collective rethinking of the professional sports' hyperproductive, corrupt economies, and the gendered dispositifs they rely upon?

And when a gesture of "humanized" treatment toward trans women and travestis in prisons is instrumentalized by Bolsonaro's Mafia through insults, it is not solely about defending individual rights independently of one's crimes, but an opportunity to promote critical perspectives on judicial rights and the prison-industrial complex and its increasingly privatized, mediatized functions; a complex that must

be linked to the extreme global extractivism, militarism, and fascism which organize violence.

I share these few thoughts in the hope of situating antigender agendas within the attempts of colonial reestablishment operating today in Brazil and Abya Yala through bio-necropolitical supremacisms and extractivisms, which in relation to data invisibilities and exotisms also interrogate the political role of the sciences. To connect these dots, especially in times of pandemia, seems critical for our collective survival and well-being.

A Church Coalition's Rainbow-Inclusion Efforts in India

Pawan Dhall

Religion does not enthrall me, but its influence on queer lives does affect me. As a queer activist working since the 1990s, I have come across people who have reconciled their religion's diktats on sin, guilt, and shame with their gender or sexuality, HIV status, or occupation in sex work. There are others, though, who remain trapped in between. In search of better ways to help them, I became familiar with faith-based organizations (FBOs) in the mid-2000s in the context of the HIV epidemic.

I was highly skeptical about their approach at first, suspecting a judgmental attitude rather than respect for human diversity.

However, in 2009, I came to know about an FBO called the National Council of Churches in India (NCCI), when they issued a statement in support of the High Court of Delhi's decision to read down Section 377 of the Indian Penal Code, a British-era law that continued to criminalize queer people even after sixty-two years of Independence. NCCI, a forum of thirty-one Protestant and Orthodox churches across India, was one of the few FBOs willing to revisit their stance on non-normative genders and sexualities, and seemingly even at the cost of upsetting member churches. Given that Section 377 was a "great religious unifier," NCCI also put themselves at risk of unshielded criticism from non-Christian organizations.

In 2016, when I attended an NCCI conference of church leaders, theologians, and queer activists at the United Theological College in Bangalore, I further learned that NCCI's ESHA program had convened workshops on human sexuality for church leaders as early as 2001, engaging queer Christians as advocates. In their centennial year of 2014, NCCI set up the National Ecumenical Forum for Gender and Sexual Diversities. They also drafted a course on human sexuality for graduate students of theology. This was rather courageous since the Supreme Court of India had just turned back the clock to reinstate Section 377—though they eventually read it down again, and irreversibly, in 2018.

NCCI now aims to transform the Ecumenical Forum into an autonomous institute for gender, sexuality, and religious equality, and to move beyond individual programs like ESHA to make NCCI's entire organizational policy queer inclusive. NCCI's efforts are thought-provoking. Hinduism as a faith and amalgam of cultures already embodies several examples of queerness. It also claims to have no queerphobic strictures comparable to those supposedly prescribed in Judeo-Christian religions. But I fear that this openness is being appropriated by queer Hindutva proponents as an unsubstantiated claim of cultural superiority, where literary research shows that queerness has a positive space in other religions as well.

I hope that NCCI's credibility as a queer-friendly FBO grows. Simultaneously, I look for greater nuance in their work. They have published a considerable amount of literature to question the belief that the Bible condemns homosexuality as a sin. Yet, some of these texts only seem to accept queer people contingent on same-sex marriage. What about single queer people?

If a kinder and more just practice of religion is possible, one that overcomes the literal adherence to scriptural divination, then a queer studies circle piloted in 2019 by Bishop's College, a Kolkata-based NCCI affiliate, comes to mind. The circle aimed to facilitate friendship between "faculty and students of theology" and "queer persons." Such an initiative might better address the post-decriminalization need for an anti-discrimination ethos and drive home the message that "homophobia is un-Christian."

The Trial of Kenya's LGBT Community in the Court of Public Opinion

Kari Mugo

As April dovetailed into May 2020, amidst an unprecedented moment in the world, the High Court in Kenya was making its ruling in a petition brought by filmmaker Wanuri Kahiu against the Kenya Film Classification Board (KFCB), the agency responsible for the national regulation of films and broadcast content. In the petition, Kahiu was challenging the KFCB's decision to ban her film *Rafiki* from viewership and distribution within the country. *Rafiki*, which means "friend" in Kiswahili, tells the coming-of-age story of a romance between two women in Nairobi's housing estates. Banned in April 2018 for, as the board put it, "its homosexual theme and clear intent to promote lesbianism in Kenya contrary to the law," the movie went on to premiere at Cannes, making history as Kenya's first feature at the festival.

Back in Kenya, the film was greeted with far less celebration. Kenya is one of dozens of countries in Africa that still has jurisdiction to criminalize consensual same-sex sexual activity. With hundreds of annual reported violations and instances of discrimination against sexual and gender minorities, the courts have emerged as a new battleground for activists and opponents in the push for human rights for LGBT people. While Kahiu's case sought to establish her constitutional right to the freedom of expression, we know that censorship of LGBT stories is one way in which discourse can be stymied, limiting the public's understanding of the challenges that the community faces, prejudicing myths and stereotypes instead. The ruling in April against Kahiu, in favor of upholding the ban, therefore came as a disappointment.

Following the judgment, the director of KFCB, an overzealous moral policeman, who once called for two male lions appearing to have sex in the Maasai Mara to receive counseling, had this to say on Twitter: "We stood for family values and what we believe to be in the best interest of Kenya. Family is the basic unit of society."

In a country where a reported 80 percent of its 47+ million-strong population identifies as Christian, "family values" has become a dog whistle for conservatism, which in Kenya includes a rejection of homosexuality, fierce admonition of abortion as a woman's right, and opposition to divorce and single parenthood. But Kahiu's case is not the first time that Christian values have been conflated with national ones, or for that matter the public's interest.

Barely a year ago, in another courtroom in the constitutional division of the High Court of Kenya, activists attempting to decriminalize same-sex conduct received another ruling laden with similar appeals. In that ruling, the court had argued that repealing Sections 162 and 165 of the Penal Code, which make same-sex conduct punishable with up to fourteen years imprisonment, would not only go against national values but threaten the basic unity of the family. Repealing these laws, the judges said, would sanction the coupling and cohabitation of same-sex individuals, posing a challenge to the constitutional definition of marriage as between members of the opposite sex. It was not enough that activists in petitions and oral submissions had argued that this case was not about the right to marry.

Both cases are under appeal and highlight the challenges in seeking redress through the courts, particularly when faced with a fervent religious block that feels mandated by the strength of its numbers to push for a religious state, where a secular one also stands.

LGBTQI of the Lebanese Revolution Don't Need Permission

Dayna Ash

The October Revolution (still ongoing) in Lebanon erupted due to cedars burning, the drop in currency value, and an exorbitant taxation placed on a failing infrastructure enabled by forty-five years of corruption.

The Lebanese Republic is governed by the Free Patriotic Movement, which is currently led by Gebran Bassil, an ex-minister and the son-in-law of the president. They propagate divisive racist, sexist, and homophobic slurs to control, demonize, and segregate the public with conservative and religious rhetoric, as indicated recently by Charbel Khalil, the director of programs at OTV, a TV channel owned and operated by the party: "Your homosexual deviance, your demons, your Mashrou' Leila WILL NOT PASS. You're dragging this country to destruction."

The LGBTQI community did not infiltrate the revolution, but neither are we on its outskirts; LGBTQI is part of what makes up society in Lebanon, ranging from capitalists to communists, from the lower class to the upper, from young women to old men, and all the in-betweens. LGBTQI are Muslim, Christian, Druze, and atheists.

While Khalil and the sectarian leaders deliberate over whether to permit LGBTQI participation in society, we live and flourish in mundane and sublime moments. We work in creative agencies, write television shows, direct films, and style your colleagues and favorite artists. We are dropping our children off at school, driving cabs, wrapping sandwiches, and working as bank tellers. The LGBTQI community is marching with mothers and fathers, with migrant workers and with refugees against classism, racism, elitism, sexism, and sectarianism, while defending the front lines with bodies and voices. LGBTQI distribute food, carry the wounded to first-aid tents, throw stones when enraged. Thousands stood shoulder to shoulder as fists penetrated the air dense with tear gas. "The Queers Built Beirut" is still etched into the concrete walls that separated the protesters from the Grand Serail.

The heart of the protests in the capital city was at the Ring, where the major highways converge. The Ring is also where the graffiti "Yas Queer" and "down with the regime" are seen side by side because they are one and the same. The highway that had once divided the country during the civil war has now been reclaimed by its free citizens: among the many revolutionaries that closed the Ring were the lesbians, trans*, gays, queers, and nonbinary activists of Lebanon. And as the public squares filled with dialogue that the system had once worked so hard to isolate, protesters listened to one another when asked to refrain

from using "gay" as a derogatory remark and "womanhood" as a weakness.

Revolution breeds clarity, and with it comes solidarity. Those that are oppressed can no longer be maligned when the same oppressor holds an iron fist over all our houses: the only time we are all considered equal is when we are subjugated to injustice and oppression. The queers are not the "unnatural" force that strangled the country but the "natural" revolution to free it from its shackles. We did not infiltrate society. We are not deductible nor an alternative. We will not fade into the background or be sedated. The revolution is not queer; the queers are a revolution.

Of Islamic Laws and the Colonial Past: The Conundrums Faced by the Malaysian LGBT Community

Niza

In September 2018, Malaysia made news for caning two women for attempting *musahaqah* (lesbian sex). The women were charged under Section 30 of the Syariah Criminal Offences Enactment 2001, read in conjunction with Section 59 (1) of the same enactment. They were fined US$800 each and caned six times in front of around 150 people in the court of the conservative state of Terengganu.

The caning was intended to humiliate. LGBT activist and friend Thilaga Sulathireh, from the group Justice for Sisters, said she wept witnessing the event. As someone who identifies as lesbian, I was shocked by the court decision, along with my fellow community of queer women. Our community stays away from provoking the authorities, meeting only here and there in secret. Many scholars state that lesbians have not posed much of a threat historically, in comparison to homosexual men.

Malaysia has two legal systems: one secular, inherited from British colonialism, and the other is a Syariah system which governs Muslims in matters such as marriage, divorce, and alimony. Both systems discriminate against LGBT people.

Malaysia's preoccupation with our community is not new. In 2008, the National Fatwa Council issued a religious edict against *pengkids* (a degrading term for women who dress like men and who may or may not have sexual desires for other women). Gay men have been sent to prison. Transgender women are routinely murdered. And online harassment of Malaysian LGBT people persists.

Malaysia is considered a "moderate Muslim nation" by many, but it has seen a rise of Islamic fundamentalism since the 1970s. Most Muslims believe that the community of Prophet Lot was condemned by God for practicing homosexuality, as described in the Qur'an. Sodomy is today outlawed under Section 377 of the Malaysian Penal Code, which was first introduced by British colonial rulers. The most famous use of this law was in 1998 when Malaysia's then prime minister, Mahathir Mohamad, sacked his deputy Anwar Ibrahim on allegations of sodomy in an attempt to destroy his career.

Yet, despite popular misconceptions, Southeast Asia, the Malay Archipelago included, has a rich history of gender and sexual diversity. Researcher Sarah Ngu asserts that Malay rulers as far back as the fifteenth century appointed *sida-sida* in their palaces. These androgynous courtiers had sex with both genders, and their role was to protect the women of the court.

Regarding the recent caning, local feminist group Sisters in Islam released a statement: "Qur'anic teachings emphasize repentance, forgiveness, and personal transformation. God is forgiving and merciful." While it may not be approving of homosexuality itself, their statement is radical. Such progressive voices are rare in Malaysia because many Muslims believe that human rights, liberalism, and pluralism go against Islam. It may take years, generations even, for Malaysian LGBT people to get their rights, but there is a glimmer of hope. I for one hope that as Malaysian society progresses, so do the rights for our marginalized community.

Love in the Time of Corona

Naoufal Bouzid

I'm not a naive, optimistic person, and I've always been proud of being rational and stoic, especially when looking at the present and what the future might hold. However, I cannot deny my feelings of loneliness during the enforced solitude in this time of Covid-19. I have also witnessed the beauty of my country, both in the solidarity of the people and the relative coherence of the government—though, realistically, this will probably only last no more than a couple of months.

A few days after the lockdown, on April 13, the Moroccan, trans-gender, Instagram-influencer Naoufal Moussa (aka SofíaTalouni) encouraged the use of location-based dating apps, usually used by gay men and often, to "out" others within the community. Many people took up their proposition and created fake profiles, then they started taking screenshots and pictures of other users and posting them on Facebook. As a result, between fifty and one hundred people were outed against their will, which caused a huge wave of hate against the LGBTQ+ community on social media.

I am talking about a community that has never learned to communicate in public or to support each other, nor the skills to fight back; there is no history of shared struggle. However, in this case the LGBTQ+ community started listing the attackers and mapping the victims, coordinating support for those who found themselves in need of assistance or a shelter. I was personally surprised to see such solidarity inside the LGBTQ+ community in Morocco. For the first time in history, this episode managed to unite all the colors of the rainbow in my country, with LGBTQ+ people reaching out to the world with their little phones, from the corners of their little houses, among families who were completely unaware of the tragedy affecting the gay community.

What Sofía did must be taken as a general lesson. It comes as a result of political decisions made over recent generations, resulting in poor education and a strong iron-fisted government, which without the will to recognize its responsibility in creating a community of cultural and sexual acceptance stops anyone courageously standing against it.

As human rights activists and engaged citizens, we don't want anything more than basic common sense and rights to an environment which will allow us to grow, so to help our country grow. I'm not a fan of victimization speeches, but I wish to see LGBTQ+ groups being able to officially register as organizations, and to no longer have to work in the shadows for fear of being caught. Being deprived of the freedom of organization, and thus of assembly, is what makes the situation here a lot worse.

I don't think I demand too much as a citizen of this country when I say I need to have the right to protect my privacy, far from the judgment of the law and away from the culture of scriptural interpretation. We are not seeking the impossible when we ask for a fundamental cultural revolution that eases the way to political and social change. Until then, I'm happy to see that the new LGBTQ+ generation has found an alternative underground solution to organizing themselves around the love they have for one another, not waiting nor caring about having the permission to fight for a better colored life.

A Trojan Horse for Warsaw's Castle

Eliel Jones

After thirty years of field-bending contemporary art programming, Ujazdowski Castle Centre for Contemporary Art (CCA) in Warsaw lost its most recent director, Małgorzata Ludwisiak, to the newly appointed Piotr Bernatowicz: a decision made by the minister of culture without an open competition, as is usually the case for public positions. That Bernatowicz is renowned for curating dubious exhibitions featuring misogynist and homophobic content and that his vision for CCA will focus on artists whose work champions conservative, patriotic, and pro-family values is a response to the last few years of activities at CCA, which

have only established the institution as a safe space for minority communities in Warsaw.

Over eighteen months alone, the resident queer and feminist collective Kem filled the castle—itself a reconstruction, once a palace—with as much nourishment as many art institutions only hope to provide after years of concerted effort. Focusing on expanded choreographic practices, Kem have managed to create an artistic infrastructure that exists alongside institutions and with their financial support. This position of being both inside and outside has allowed the collective to realize projects such as their temporary queer summer *Dragana Bar* in 2018 at CCA, which they removed a window from the castle's facade to build, replacing it with a set of metal doors and a stairway that facilitated autonomous activity during opening times that extended well beyond the castle's usual public hours.

To see the hundreds of people pour in and out of this parasitic architecture over the summer of *Dragana* was to bear witness to a resistance to the country's control over the behavior, aesthetics, and gender-fucking presentation of unruly bodies. For Poland's governing party Law and Justice (PiS), the very fact of being LGBT+ goes against the idea (by the Catholic church's moral standing) of a valuable and (re)productive member of Polish society. In asserting a space for self-affirmation, as much as dissent, Kem helped fracture the homogeneity that is at the core of PiS's project of a unified (singular and same) Poland.

Equally jostling with the new director's vision was the recent retrospective *The Power of Secrets* (November 15, 2019–March 29, 2020) by Warsaw-based queer artist Karol Radziszewski, who founded Queer Archives Institute and *DIK Fagazine*: two world-making projects that render visible the lives and stories of queer persons in Eastern Europe. When it was known that Bernatowicz would be taking over the institution, curator Michał Grzegorzek and others established a new clause in the artist's contract, stating that any attempt to censor or close the exhibition prior to its planned duration would result in legally binding financial compensation to the artist.

This preemptive effort is but one example of the local and international art community's myriad attempts to stop the appointment of Bernatowicz, or at least, failing that, to challenge his tenure. But the castle's fort will only hold for so long. Some of CCA's key staff have already taken up positions elsewhere. Those that remain fight micro battles daily, such as the censorship of the recent "Anti-fascism for the Unconvinced" program. Kem too have recently forged alliances with Krytyka Polityczna (Political Critique), a Pan-European online magazine and activist group who, much like the Trojans, sought substantial funding from the City of Warsaw. Kem are currently developing an experimental queer and feminist education program—the first of its kind in Poland—as part of this initiative, which will be open and free to all as of 2021. Though the castle may have fallen, it seems that this will not be the last chance to rebuild it again.

AROUND

Documentation and analysis that places current against nature laws in historical context. Legal scholars guide us through the most influential cases of anti-sodomy law.

A HISTORICAL VERDICT

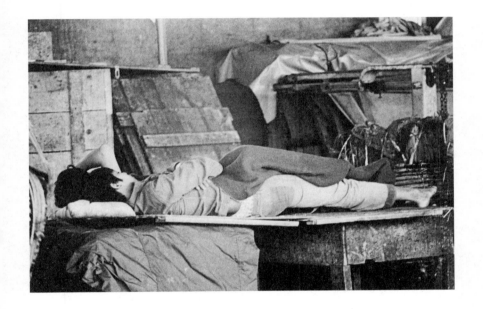

DOCUMENT

Published in SCC Online® and reproduced with the kind permission of EBC Publishing Pvt. Ltd., Lucknow, India.

1924 SCC ONLINE SIND JC 49 : AIR 1925 SIND 286
KHANU V. EMPEROR
IN THE COURT OF JUDICIAL COMMISSIONER, SIND

(Before Kincaid, J.C. and Kennedy, A.J.C.)

Khanu . . . Appellant;
Versus
Emperor . . . Opposite Party.

Criminal Appeal No. 15 of 1924
Decided on April 28, 1924

JUDGMENT

1. The principal point in this case is whether the accused (who is clearly guilty of having committed the sin of Gomorrah *coitus per os*) with a certain little child, the innocent accomplice of his abomination, has thereby committed an offence under S. 377, Indian Penal Code, 1860.

2. S. 377 punishes certain persons who have carnal intercourse against the order of nature with *inter alia* human beings. Is the act here committed one of carnal intercourse? If so, it is clearly against the order of nature, because the natural object of carnal intercourse is that there should be the possibility of conception of human beings, which in the case of *coitus per os* is impossible. Intercourse may be defined as mutual frequent action by members of independent organisation. Commercial intercourse provides for the merchants of the state *A* who wish to come to and trade in the state *B*, not intending permanently to settle there but with *animus redcandi* to *A*, and similarly for the merchants of the state *B*. Such is the *magnus* intercourse which regulated the trade of Britain and Flanders in the middle ages. Social intercourse provides the rules under which members of one family may resort to the premises occupied by another family, not intending to reside in such premises occupied by another family, not intending to reside in such premises but merely to visit them for laudable purposes, reciprocity being, of the essence of the bargain. By a metaphor the word intercourse, like the word commerce, is applied to the relations of the sexes. Here also there is the temporary visitation of one organism by a member of the other organisation, for certain clearly defined and limited objects. The primary object of the visiting organisation

is to obtain euphoria by means of a detent of the nerves conse-
quent on the sexual crisis. But there is no intercourse unless the
visiting member is enveloped at least partially by the visited
organism, for intercourse connotes reciprocity. Looking at the
question in this way, it would seem that sin of Gomorrah is no
less carnal intercourse than the sin of Sodom. The sin of Lesbos
or Reboim is clearly not such intercourse, and I doubt if mutual
cheirourgia would be such. Not very much can be gathered from
a consideration of English authorities, which are all affected by
the fact that the offence of unnatural vice was originally one of
the three offences dealt with by the ecclesiastical tribunals and
that the Civil Courts, when called on to deal with those offences,
showed their usual tendency to look with much jealousy on
the criminal legislation of the church. The cognate offences of
heresy and usury are now not dealt with by the Criminal Courts
at all, and the third is held only to have been committed when
the offender is proved to have committed the sin of Sodom. And
it was this vice in particular which was rendered punishable by
the early Christian state, for it was par excellence the vice of the
Hellene and the Saracen. By making this vice particularly pun-
ishable, therefore, the State not only protected good moral but
struck at its enemies. It is this vice, therefore, which attracted
severest censures of State and Church, but in mediaeval times all
emission other than in *vas legitimum* was considered unchris-
tian because such emission was supposed ultimately to cause
conception of demons.

3. It will be seen how little help can be extracted from
Christian sources in deciding this question. But why is it that
most modern States, now freed from the influence of supersti-
tion, still make the sin of Sodom punishable. Partly I suppose
of the desire of princes to encourage legitimate marriage. Partly
because there is an idea, (perhaps erroneous) that the public
tolerated practice of that vice creates a tendency in the citizens
of the State, where it is practiced, to adopt an unmanly and mor-
bid method of life and thinking, so that a person saturated with
those ideas is less useful a member of society. Partly because of
the danger that men put in authority over other men may use
their power for the gratification of their lusts. But principally
I suppose because of the danger to young persons, lest they be
indoctrinated into sexual matters prematurely. But surely all
these ill consequences would equally follow in a city where the
sin of Gomorrah was tolerated.

4. It is to be remembered that the Penal Code does not, except in S. 377, render abnormal sexual vice punishable at all. In England indecent assaults are punishable very severely. It is possible that under the Penal Code, some cases might be met by prosecuting the offender for simple assault, but that is a compoundable offence and in any case the patient could in no way be punished. Is it to be supposed that the Legislature intended that a Tigellinus should carry on his nefarious profession perhaps vitiating and depraving hundreds of children with perfect immunity?

5. I doubt not, therefore, that *coitus per os* is punishable under S. 377, Indian Penal Code, 1860.

6. But we must not allow our disgust at the perpetrators of such acts to blind us to the fact that this vice is less pernicious than the sin of Sodom. It has not been surrounded by the halo of art, eloquence, and poetry. It cannot be practised on persons who are unwilling. It is not common and can never be so. It cannot produce the physical changes which the other vice produces. It is, therefore, rightly punishable but the punishment need not be so extremely severe as in the other case.

7. Neither the actual penetration *per annus* or in a legal sense attempt at such penetration is proved in the present case.

8. As for the question of kidnapping, the learned Judge has not addressed himself to that question with his usual thoroughness. It is arguable that a child playing in the street and induced to accompany a man for a few minutes is not kidnapped; it would be otherwise no doubt if there were a diversion, *e.g.*, if the child had been intercepted while going to school or sent on some errand. But on the other hand, the child next was locked up, and thus wholly put under the dominion of the accused. Thus it would seem there was a kidnapping. I would, therefore, dismiss the appeal against the convictions under Ss. 367 and 377 and against the sentence under S. 367. But I would reduce the sentence under S. 377 to one of 5 years' rigorous imprisonment. The sentences to be concurrent.

9. *Appeal dismissed.*

ESSAY

Grappling with the "Unnatural": A Dubious Judicial History

Vivek Divan

UNENLIGHTENED PREJUDICE

One of the first significant interpretations of the British law that was imposed in India in 1860, and several British colonies thereafter—the odious Section 377 of the Indian Penal Code—was provided by Justices Kincaid and Kennedy in Sindh (now Pakistan) in the 1924 judgment of Khanu v. Emperor.

Section 377 reads as follows:

> *377. Unnatural offences.—*
> *Whoever voluntarily has carnal intercourse against the order of nature with any man, woman or animal, shall be punished with imprisonment for life, or with imprisonment of either description for a term which may extend to ten years, and shall also be liable to fine.*
>
> *Explanation —*
> *Penetration is sufficient to constitute the carnal intercourse necessary to the offence described in this section.*

What is clear and does not require judicial interpretation is that a kind of sex ("carnal intercourse") was punishable even if it was consensual ("voluntarily") between adults ("whoever" with "man, woman . . ."). But the question of what was "unnatural" as per the title of the section and what was "against the order of nature" was up for interpretation. Its meaning vexed many a judge for over a century. In the report of 2008 "This Alien Legacy: The Origins of 'Sodomy' Laws in British Colonialism," Human Rights Watch covers much of this judicial contemplation.[1]

What judges of yore felt about "the order of nature" and "unnaturalness" in regard to sexual intercourse became particularly important in the public domain when a concerted effort challenging the constitutional validity of Section 377 took place in India from 2001 onward. An entire community of queer individuals, activists, and their allies from the sexuality, HIV, and other movements made this challenge successful. The Delhi High Court struck down the law as it pertained to consensual sex between adults in 2009.[2] A travesty of justice was to follow a few years later, however. In 2013, the Supreme Court of India countenanced an appeal (made in large part by religious hard-liners of Hindu, Muslim, and Christian persuasions) of the earlier decision: gay sex was recriminalized and Section 377 was back in play. Fortunately, after realizing that a mockery had been made of the constitutional rights of queer people, the Supreme Court reversed its decision in 2018. Today "unnatural" sex is legal in India as it pertains to consenting adults.

But what is this sex that is "against the order of nature"? The Khanu decision is where one begins to see the judiciary grappling with this term in earnest.[3] Although court rulings are hard to fathom for nonlawyers at the best of times, the Khanu judgment is hard reading for a lawyer too. For a lawyer who is agnostic/atheist it is even more challenging.

Although no more than two pages in length, the judgment held forth on the "order of nature" in a most protracted manner, replete with Judeo-Christian references that revealed the colonial domination and morality that India was oppressed by as well as understandings of sexuality that were ignorant at best. Khanu was a case involving the sexual abuse of a minor. Yet, this fact (that the case involved a person incapable of giving consent in law) appears to have played no role in making the court indignant. What the court was engrossed with was whether the act of the accused (oral sex) amounted to "carnal intercourse against the order of nature." The court held that it did. As the "natural object of carnal intercourse is that there should be the possibility of conception of human beings," oral sex was "unnatural."[4]

With what was evidently great abhorrence and appears to have been abject discomfort in dealing with issues of sexual intercourse and sexuality, the judges traversed the meaning of "intercourse," using the metaphor of commerce and trade to describe it. And, in describing sexual intercourse they elucidated on the notion of "penetration" in Section 377:

> a temporary visitation by one organism by a member of the other organization, for certain clearly defined and limited objects. The

*primary object of the visiting organism is to
obtain euphoria by means of a detente of the
nerves consequent on the sexual crisis. But
there is no intercourse unless the visiting
member is enveloped at least partially by the
visited organism, for intercourse connotes
reciprocity.*

*Looking at the question this way it would
seem that the sin of Gomorrah is no less car-
nal than the sin of Sodom. The sin of Lesbos
or Reboim is clearly not such intercourse,
and I doubt if mutual* cheirourgia *[mastur-
bation] would be such.*[5]

As Human Rights Watch points out, Section
377 was an imposition of British Christian values, having
nothing to do with Indian society and its mores. The coloniz-
ers saw Indians as degenerate, to be reined in.[6] Indeed, this
legal provision became "a colonial attempt to set standards
of behavior, both to reform the colonized and to protect the
colonizers against moral lapses,"[7] and a model to be emulated
in other British colonies, particularly in Asia and Africa.[8]

The Khanu judgment revealed a lot more,
laced as it was with Christian preeminence and overt racism:
the "unnatural . . . vice in particular . . . was rendered pun-
ishable by the Christian state, for it was par excellence the
vice of the Hellene and the Saracen [Greeks and Arabs]."[9]
Inexplicable personal predilections revealed themselves in
the assessment that oral sex—even when it involved a mi-
nor—was less malevolent than anal sex: "It cannot be prac-
ticed on persons who are unwilling. It is not common and can
never be so. It cannot produce the physical changes which
the other vice produces. It is, therefore, rightly punishable,
but the punishment need not be so extremely severe."[10]

Judicial ignorance was revealed in Khanu
through the observation that the "sin of Sodom" (anal sex)
is still punished in "modern States" due to "danger to young
persons, lest they be indoctrinated into sexual matters
prematurely,"[11] thus reinforcing the false link between ho-
mosexual sex and child sexual abuse. Of course, the lan-
guage of Section 377 allowed for the lumping together of
these acts, along with bestiality, while consent between
adults was of no consequence.

While the courts pre-independence reflected
the foreign morality demonstrated in Khanu, tragically
judges in free India were all too happy to ape the colonizers.
A series of judgments after Independence in 1947 followed in
the same vein. Based on the belief that non-procreative sex
was "unnatural," these rulings reiterated that Section 377
covered acts of oral sex[12] and included acts that imitated
penetration (thrusting the penis between thighs[13] or mutual
masturbation[14]). As has been rightly observed, "judges tried
to bring an ever wider range of sexual acts within the laws'
punitive reach: descending while doing it, into almost-com-
ical obsessions with orifice and organ, desire and detail."[15]

DISINGENUOUS CONFLATION

Until recently, the devious imagery of child sexual abuse and
homosexuality was irresponsibly bandied about by parties
before the court and the judges hearing the cases that chal-
lenged the validity of Section 377. When the Indian govern-
ment filed its affidavit in 2003 it evoked just these falsehoods,
stating that delinquent behavior would be unleashed on soci-
ety if the law were removed. During proceedings in court its
lawyers constantly reiterated this falsehood. This was partic-
ularly irksome given that the petitioners and the queer com-
munity that litigated the case had been conscious that Section
377 was the only law in India then which could be deployed in
cases of child sexual abuse. They thereby asked that the section
be retained for such situations, but be interpreted ("read
down") henceforth to exclude consensual sex between adults.
        The drumbeat of lies, however, appeared to
have worked. One of the Supreme Court judges who recrim-
inalized gay sex in 2013 later stated that the material on child
pornography which was placed before the court weighed
heavily on his mind.[16] Presumably, the judge was giving this
as an excuse for his perverse verdict. Yet, if one reads that
judgment and its flimsy reasoning, nowhere will such a jus-
tification be found.[17]

CODA—THE VAGARIES OF JUSTICE

The 2013 judgment took the queer community back to the dark
ages of colonized India. Moreover, it was sketchy in its analysis

and understanding of many legal principles, including that of judicial review and even the workings of democracy. A reading of the judgment reveals very little about the substance of Section 377. And all the evidence placed before the court on how this law oppressed queer lives was entirely ignored. What the decision also disguises rather well is the palpable discomfort that the judges exhibited while hearing the case.

That unease with matters of sex and sexuality is partly revealed in the transcript of the entire proceedings.[18] But it was best experienced by being present in the courtroom, where one could witness the many sidelong glances and grimaces that the judges made at each other, and the frequent fidgeting in their seats when such matters were raised. Their lowbrow comments and flippant humor about sexual intercourse were attempts to lighten the courtroom atmosphere and alleviate their embarrassment. For example, that homosexuality may or may not be normal: "we can't say, only persons with experience can say so."[19] Or absurd extensions of logic that obfuscated the issues at hand: "Would breastfeeding come within the meaning of carnal intercourse?"[20]

On repeated questioning by the judges for the meaning of "carnal intercourse" and "against the order of nature," the lawyers appearing on behalf of queer people constantly and painstakingly explained the phrases. Yet, the court was dissatisfied. It countered claims made by these lawyers, stating that Section 377 did not criminalize a sexual orientation but only sexual acts, and that these acts could also be between heterosexuals. Failing to recognize how the law disproportionately impacted queer lives, irrespective of the meaning of these phrases, the court sought to put into question whether Section 377 in any way affected queer people in their constitutional claims to life, liberty, privacy, and equality. Queerphobia manifested in the courtroom over those several days of argumentation in 2013, ultimately leading to the revival of Section 377 in its full force.

Fortunately, this ruling was overturned in 2018 and queer people were finally decriminalized. Luck— which should not be the basis of justice—had a significant role to play, as it did in 2009 when the law was first read down, and in 2013 when it was upheld. The luck was in having the right judges (in 2009 and 2018) and the wrong ones (in 2013) hear the case. In both instances when the law was read down, the judges who heard the case knew or had met and engaged with queer people. The justices of 2013 had in fact met queer people

through their affidavits submitted to court.[21] But they refused
to engage with and understand what was squarely placed be-
fore them; not once did they refer to these testimonies in their
lengthy judgment, which was a dereliction of duty and cow-
ardice at play. At one point during the hearings, the judges
even asked the lawyer arguing the case whether he knew any-
one who was gay.[22] Many of us queers present were stupefied
and some of us were left in a quandary — would it be appropri-
ate to Bollywoodize this moment in the hallowed portals of
the Supreme Court and stand up to be counted in a context
where such swagger is looked down with disdain?[23]

       That moment was one among many during
those hearings, which reflected a court and an establishment
that was out of touch with social realities. One way in which
the 2018 ruling has dealt with this disconnect is to ask the
Indian government to take "all measures to ensure that this
judgment is given wide publicity through the public media"
and initiate programs to remove the stigma associated with
queer people.[24] The government has done no such thing. If it
ever did, a greater number of people would more fully under-
stand the true subjectivity of nature.

NOTES

[1]
Human Rights Watch, "This Alien Legacy: The Origins of 'Sodomy' Laws in British Colonialism" (December 2008), accessed April 14, 2020, https://www.hrw.org/sites/default/files/reports/lgbt1208_webwcover.pdf.

[2]
Naz Foundation v. Government of National Capital Territory of Delhi (2009), Delhi High Court, https://indiankanoon.org/doc/100472805.

[3]
Prior to this, courts considered the phrase to mean "anal sex": "the act must be in that part where sodomy is usually committed." Government v. Bapoji Bhatt (1884), Mysore Law Reports, vol. 7.

[4]
Khanu v. Emperor (1925), High Court of Sindh, 286, para. 2.

[5]
Ibid.

[6]
Human Rights Watch, "This Alien Legacy," 1, 10.

[7]
Ibid., 5.

[8]
Ibid.

[9]
Khanu v. Emperor, para. 2.

[10]
Khanu v. Emperor, para. 6.

[11]
Khanu v. Emperor, para. 3.

[12]
Lohana Vasantlal Devchand v. State (1968), A.I.R., Gujarat, 252.

[13]
State of Kerala v. K. Govindan (1969), Cr. L.J, 818.

[14]
Brother John Antony v. State (1992), Cr. L.J, 124.

[15]
Human Rights Watch, "This Alien Legacy," 11.

[16]
Apurva Vishwanath, "Child Porn Weighed on My Mind, Says Supreme Court Judge Who Upheld Section 377 in 2013," The Print, September 18, 2018, accessed April 14, 2020, https://theprint.in/india/governance/child-porn-weighed-on-my-mind-says-supreme-court-judge-who-upheld-section-377-in-2013/119898.

[17]
Suresh Kumar Koushal v. Naz Foundation (2013), Supreme Court of India, https://indiankanoon.org/doc/58730926.

[18]
"Notes of Proceedings in Suresh Kumar Koushal v. Naz Foundation" (2012), Supreme Court of India, accessed April 14, 2020, http://orinam.net/377/wp-content/uploads/2013/12/SC_Transcripts_Hearings.pdf.

[19]
Ibid., 15.

[20]
Ibid., 104.

[21]
Parth Khatau, "Courts Are There to Exercise a Restraining Influence on Authority: Justice Chandrachud," Indian Express, February 10, 2019, accessed April 14, 2020, https://indianexpress.com/article/cities/mumbai/courts-are-there-to-exercise-a-restraining-influence-on-authority-justice-chandrachud-5576855.

[22]
Anoo Bhuyan, "How 'Unconvicted Felons' Stood in the Supreme Court and Watched Section 377 Fall," The Wire, September 9, 2018, accessed April 14, 2020, https://thewire.in/lgbtqia/section-377-decriminalisation-lgbtq-supreme-court.

[23]
Vivek Divan, "We queer people will do everything to ensure our liberty, even if it takes some Bollywoodising," February 1, 2016, accessed April 14, 2020, https://scroll.in/article/802812/we-queer-people-will-do-everything-to-ensure-our-liberty-even-if-it-takes-some-bollywoodising.

[24]
Navtej Singh Johar v. Union of India Ministry of Law (2018), Supreme Court of India, https://indiankanoon.org/doc/168671544.

THE MAGIC OF

A guiding force within the LGBTQI+ community in Africa. The life and work of Binyavanga Wainaina inspires reflections on what it means to believe, write, and think through sexuality and spirituality.

BINYAVANGA WAINAINA

STORY

How to Binj

Amatesiro Dore

I

We're at the Coast of Sierra Leone. The weather is like steam rising from a boiling kettle. Pores are open, and sweat is welcome. Unlike cooler places where sweat has the flavor of something fermented, here, it is the sheen of every limb. Sweat is only a perfume when fresh, free-flowing. It is the only air-conditioner that works.

Cold things, iced things are silly here. They just give you the false illusion that you are chilled, before heat overwhelms you with a vengeance.

Pots stir in the midday heat. The kitchen is in the court-yard, kids are playing. Somebody is grinding chili. I have often wondered why chilis get hotter the hotter a place is. To get you to sweat, I guess.

From the Congo River to Nigeria, palates embrace musk and any other flavors that mimic the most sensual smells of the body. Yams. If potatoes ever were in heat, this is what they would taste like.

—Binyavanga Wainaina, "Prawn Palaver" (ca. 2001)

The Binj was a cook, and his favorite ingredients were words that produced imagery. His father, Job Muigai Wainaina, was the founding managing director of a Kenyan government para-statal; his mother, Rosemary Kankindi, was a hairdresser, mother of four, with Ugandan and Rwandan bloodlines, and a periodic Pentecostal. The upper-middle-class family lived as one of the most illustrious families in Nakuru. The Binj's father abstained from looting public funds, chaired the local golf club, and managed a private farming enterprise to sponsor the cosmopolitan education of his children.

The Binj was loved. He was blessed with a doting mother and a compassionate father, who was easily manipulated by his children. That love became the seed that blossomed into the charitable lifestyle of the Binj. He performed the life of a savior, serving as an unsolicited literary agent of African writers; he was the number one referee for grants, scholarships, and residencies long before he was named one of *Time* magazine's 100 Most Influential People in 2014. It was boring old love for Africa and Africans that drove his life and career. From cradle to grave.

The Binj was a failure who tried to make success out of everything and for everyone in Africa, starting with food. He looked inward and commenced the process of exhibiting African excellence at the heart of Africa, South Africa. His contemporary Chimamanda Ngozi Adichie immigrated to America for tertiary education, like other upper-middle-class kids, while the Binj went to the best place within the continent. The Binj cooked after failing in school and tried to run an African catering business (while he wrote on the side, gathering hundreds of recipes and publishing outstanding food criticism). He failed beautifully. The business never made a profit. But he was serially published in two prestigious magazines in South Africa (*Weekend Argus* and the *Sunday Times*), and went on to win the Caine Prize for African Writing in the same year that Chimamanda was short-listed.

The Binj was the second male African writer of his generation to explode from the continent after Helon Habila, another struggling writer who made it big after winning the Caine Prize. Then he performed another act of magic: he set up the magazine *Kwani?* and published Yvonne Adhiambo Owuor, whose story subsequently won the 2003 Caine Prize. He loved to be local, African, so he did not understand the Afropolitanism of Taiye Selasi and lashed out against her 2005 essay about African identity in the diaspora. He would later recant and apologize. But I doubt if he ever regretted rejecting the World Economic Forum's Young Global Leader honor. The Binj preferred to sponsor emerging African talents with food and intoxication.

After food, he profiled soccer, and Western NGO behavior on the continent. "How to Write About Africa," the Binj's classic essay, was originally a letter to the editor of *Granta* magazine, castigating their 1994 issue on Africa. He developed the rhythms of his first book, *One Day I Will Write about This Place*, during his years of curating

African cuisine across the continent. While profiling food, he also profiled talents via exquisite emails and his reliable word-of-mouth. Careers have been made on his recommendations, as a thousand tributes testify online. In a series of YouTube videos *We Must Free Our Imaginations*, you will find his motivations and why he insisted on original people and abilities, no photocopies.

The Binj was loveable. He would assemble and fund a feast of talented creatives whenever he entered any territory. He was a sugar daddy with a conscience. Having spent his twenties as an African food connoisseur and instigator of enjoyment, the rising homophobia and general conservatism spreading across the continent by Christian Pentecostals motivated his tirades against religious oppressors. He believed that New-Age Pentecostalism corrupted the faith of friends and loved ones. The personal fueled his public utterances.

Unlike his mother, he did not hear the Pentecostal God and did not regard African men of God. His god was a sci-fi, African ancestor consulting with spirits and technology. He believed that the proclamations of a Pentecostal pastor had convinced his mother not to vote in a multiparty system election; the pastor supported a one-party state government, despite evidence of wanton corruption and economic hardship in Kenya. He also believed that the reign of Pentecostal Christianity robbed Africans of original creative thinking and development. The church ascribed governmental failures and personal inadequacies to demons and so-called demonic activities. It was, for him, the very enemy of the people because it blocked their imagination. Some Pentecostal pastors in Kenya further believed they could "eradicate homosexuality" with government policies. The Binj compared their homophobia to the Salem witch trials. In an episode of *We Must Free Our Imaginations*, he says, "give me the book about demonology and how demonology is important for building roads, schools, and imagination . . . give me data . . . give me data that homosexuality is such a problem that is spreading virally."

The Pentecostals made living in Africa difficult for the Binj. He railed against them. This was why he addressed his deceased mother and her generation of Pentecostal Kenyans in his coming-out essay, "I am a Homosexual, Mum."

II

There are times that even Graham believes the story he has peddled for so many years, about how he came to be gay. That he had always known; that he used to dress up in his mother; that he had been riveted by the biceps of Mohammed Ali, the anger of those black panthers on television; that he had played the kerfuffle game in public school; that the old gay friends of his mother, who had hosted him when she was in rehab, or consulting her guru in Lucknow, had made it easy to see possibilities in this world. These things are all true, but only small accessories to the main event.

But the main event, as seen by him now, is also untruthful: it was not as clear a sexual selection as he prefers to imagine, and he knows this enough not to share this story—it could well be that he was always gay, and that he would have come to it in one way or another, despite his self-protests to the contrary. But the unambiguous epiphany that the first gay fuck gave him marked not his sexuality, but his approach to life itself, it was his Woodstock, his civil rights movement. And inside himself, he remains unconvinced of his visceral homosexuality, believes that he has willfully created himself.

—Binyavanga Wainaina, "Alien Taste" (2016)

Very few times was homosexuality the main event in the Binj's writing. In the story "Alien Taste," he compared the naturalness of queer sex to drinking beer. In his TEDGlobal 2007 talk, he said, "the most consumed stories in Africa were from the Bible." He began to rewrite Africa by challenging the dominant homophobic narrative with his imagination. At the time of his Lannan Foundation conversation with Chimamanda in 2011, he had not published any queer literature, neither had he come out, so it was fascinating to watch him discuss her *The Shivering*, a Pentecostal queer story. During the dialogue, she said, "by the time we knew he was gay, we already liked him." The Binj winced and complained about the dearth of queer literature from the continent. Then he continued to hide himself until many years later.

Pentecostalism also robbed the Binj of his mother. She believed in miraculous healing and stopped taking the necessary medication for her diabetes. It led to her death before he could come out to her. After he did come out, he was invited as a guest of honor to his prestigious Kenyan high school, but on his arrival the ceremony was canceled on the counsel of an influential bishop of the church — the church first attacked the Binj before he attacked the homophobia and intolerance of the church. In a statement reported by *The Nairobian*, he said: "Oh! There is a lot of money in gay business . . . but if I wanted real money, I would start a church. First, I would make noise against the church, then I would wait for six months and go to the biggest church in Africa and 'confess' . . . Then I would marry a beautiful musician and be featured in all the cool press in Africa: 'Meet Mr. Binyavanga and Mrs. Binyavanga, ex-homosexual and his model girlfriend sitting on a yacht . . . that is the life.'"

The Binj did not perform friendship, rather he was a friend indeed. He befriended ordinary Africans doing extraordinary things across the continent, from chauffeurs to cooks in Tanzania and Ghana, to street artists and merchants in Nairobi and Accra. Regular folks had his intercontinental phone number; everyone had direct access via his email, and he sent money for the mothers of his friends. Their pain was thereby accessible to him, and the injuries inflicted by the church on his friends stayed acute in his memory. When a church in Kenya excommunicated the mother of a late queer friend and the local community turned on the family of his deceased compatriot, he spoke back against the church. He castigated the public list of queer people authored by church-sponsored homophobes and denounced the state-endorsed discrimination against LGBTQI communities in Kenya.

When he authored his coming-out piece addressed to his late mother (and other aggrieved mothers in Kenya), he came out for a generation and interrogated the most homophobic powers in Africa: the church and the state. It was a verbal hammer to chip away at their influence. He also wanted to turn the eyes of the church away from the bedroom activities of his friends — why was the church so concerned with the sexual activities of his friends anyway? The Binj also named names and mentioned the individual homophobic bodies and personalities behind the murder, assault, and harassment of queer folks. The Binj spoke out at every opportunity and instance, challenging the homophobic churches in Kenya into a test of holiness, righteousness, and patriotism.

The Binj was a great writer, who happened to be gay. He wrote queer literature as a response to homophobia. He fought for his friends against state actors and known enemies of their lives. He was loyal to a fault because he also adopted the personal enemies of his friends, irrespective of whether his friends were wrong or not. He would have spoken out against Islam if it were part of the Pentecostal forces tormenting the health and freedom of his friends. After he came out, the Binj befriended the queer with his works and imaginations. He was not a conventional human rights activist. He had no regard for donor funds and despised the activities of Western NGOs focused on solving African problems. At the end of his life, he began to build the coalition of Upright People to stand against injustice and discrimination on the continent. He was not against a structural approach. He was simply against neocolonial Western approaches that propagate the image of a benevolent West with sinister motives. He was simple in his takedowns and tirades against homophobic Pentecostal churches in Kenya. He was not against Pentecostalism. He was against homophobia and homophobic Pentecostals who used their power to torment his friends.

III

Hey mum. I was putting my head on her shoulder, that last afternoon before she died. She was lying on her hospital bed. Kenyatta. Intensive Care. Critical Care. There. Because this time I will not be away in South Africa, fucking things up in that chaotic way of mine. I will arrive on time, and be there when she dies. My heart arrives on time.

I am holding my dying mother's hand. I am lifting her hand. Her hand will be swollen with diabetes. Her organs are failing. Hey mum. Ooooh. My mind sighs. My heart! I am whispering in her ear. She is awake, listening, soft calm loving, with my head right inside in her breathspace. She is so big—my mother, in this world, near the next world, each breath slow, but steady, as it should be. Inhale. She can carry everything. I will whisper, louder, in my minds-breath. To hers. She will listen, even if she doesn't hear. Can she?

—Binyavanga Wainaina, "I am a Homosexual, Mum" (2014)

The Binj never came out to his parents. He imagined coming out to his mum in the piece above. "Sometimes I feel like your parents are hostage to you much more than you are hostage to them, and so, the fear of, sort of, wounding them, for me, I think, was a big thing. But then, this is the opportunity to test their hearts the way I didn't give myself the opportunity to test their hearts," the Binj said to *NPR* on the publication of his essay "I am a Homosexual, Mum." In the essay, he takes us on his metamorphosis from shy to outspoken advocate of sexual rights and identities. He addressed parents, the basic unit of society, because he needed them to fight homophobia and homophobic institutions. He wanted Pentecostal parents to speak up like Bishop Christopher Senyonjo, an African hero of faith from his mother's country, who preached against the homophobic gospel of his contemporaries and the church in Uganda.

The Binj wanted to create a world of "upright people," which he defined as "people who love Africa." He embraced upright people, irrespective of race, nationality, creed, or sexuality. He wanted an Africa where all people were welcome. He wanted a safe passage across the continent. He was committed to African unity, and he extended an invitation to the Nigerian president who signed the anti-queer bill into law. The possibilities of his own death broadened his empathy to forgive across the homophobic divide. His Upright movement required the cooperation and participation of all lovers of Africa. As the effects of multiple strokes and speech impediment slowed his body, his mind expanded into using previously unconsidered mechanisms to eradicate hate from the continent.

The Binj struggled to finish his love letter to Nigeria and the continent at large. It remained a work in progress at the time of his death. It was his dying work and labor of love for the continent. He wanted to interview the political youth of the next generation. He wanted to hear their voice and document their thoughts about his Upright movement. He was against "NGO funded youth." He wanted to work with "political young people who live and survive the way the other citizens of their countries do." On his intended tour across Africa, he wanted to live with upright people. In a YouTube video statement published on his Facebook page, he said, "it could be the person I am to stay with is a homophobe. That is OK because he signed up as an upright person. In Soweto, or in Kano, or in Juba, he is responsible for our security because upright people do not allow their guests to stay where it is not safe." He could rely on the humanity of homophobes because he recalled how upright Africans across the continent rallied to raise US$30,000 to cater for his medical bills; contributors from various demographics attended fundraising drives in Lagos and Nairobi. The Binj could rally the people.

The Binj asked for donations to fund the Upright movement from ordinary Africans on the Internet. He utilized social media to rally his flock, but his failing health discouraged many supporters. He grew religious and began to explore traditional African faith healers. He patronized a *sangoma*, "a person who helps people to get in touch with their ancestors," who encouraged him to return to Kenya. In his home country, weakened by multiple sicknesses, he tried to build his coalition of Upright Africans. He ignored the homophobic Pentecostals and came to believe that the failure to recognize his ancestors was responsible for his strokes. He became quite spiritual during his last days and believed the practice of nondiscriminatory African spirituality was a pathway to a continent free of homophobia.

In the words of Adriaan van Klinken from his book *Kenyan, Christian, Queer: Religion, LGBT Activism, and Arts of Resistance in Africa*, the Binj was "a queer among the prophets." The Binj was self-appointed to lead, as in the Book of Jeremiah 1:10, "over nations and kingdoms to uproot and tear down, to destroy and overthrow, to build and to plant." Like Christ, the Binj intended to tear down the church and rebuild it without homophobia. If you dismiss his faith as the epitome of a sick body, the Binj authored a short story "Binguni!"as early as 1996 about a protagonist in an African afterlife, featuring ancestors from an Internet realm. In the story, the protagonist went to a liberal paradise, and the Binj sought the same at the end of his life.

At the time of his death, the Binj was scheduled to publish two books: *How to Write about Africa* and *It*

Is Only a Matter of Acceleration Now. According to *The Bookseller*, the first book stems from a satirical piece he wrote for *Granta* magazine in 2005, and the second book is "based on travels and interviews across Africa, aspiring to change readers' perceptions of Africa in the way V. S. Naipaul's *A Million Mutinies Now* did with India." Multiple strokes made the respectively 2017 and 2019 publication dates unfeasible. His death in Nairobi at 10 pm on May 21, 2019, ended his journey, but his works will always inspire a generation.

FICTION

Binguni!
Binyavanga Wainaina

A Note on the Story
Achal Prabhala

"Binguni!" was Binyavanga Wainaina's first pub-
lished work of fiction. He wrote it in 1996, and it
was published that same year on a now defunct
website for new writing called Pure Fiction. In 2017,
after battling multiple strokes and a range of phys-
ical problems that left him dispirited, Binyavanga
wrote to me to ask for help in finding this story.
This is the email he originally sent:

> The first short story I ever wrote was in
> 1995 or 1996. It could have been as early
> as 1993 or 1994. It was set in a heaven
> where African Ancestors went to die.
> I am desperate to find it. I remember
> the lead character was called Jango.
> There was a sentence in it about his
> mind being like a "helium balloon." It
> was published on a website that mostly
> American writers frequented. It was
> called purification.com. Is there no
> way of recovering it?

After a futile week of searching through
a range of water purification websites (thanks to
his hazy memory), I fell down a rabbit hole and
then (thanks to the great and wonderful Internet
Archive) somewhat miraculously found pure-
fiction.com, which turned out to be a surprisingly
vibrant and global hub for new writing in the mid-
1990s. And there, lying tucked away in a forgotten
corner of the archived version of the website, was
the object of his desire.

Reading it in 2017 was magical for him —
and for me. Binyavanga's broadsides against the
Pentecostal church are well known: he railed
against it in print and every other format available
to him, especially in the course of his public com-
ing out in 2014. A somewhat less-known fact about

his last years is that he became deeply invested in pagan African spirituality. It made sense. His coming out as a homosexual was followed by a series of devastating health setbacks, and this spiritual quest fit into a much larger quest—for both liberating himself from the past and attaching himself to a new emotional and intellectual core. But it also didn't make sense. Binyavanga was, for most of his life, the least spiritual person I knew.

To rediscover "Binguni!" with him was a revelation, not merely for the sheer beauty of the words but as much for learning about the person he had always been. Every single thing he spent his last years on Earth being consumed by (spirituality, sexuality, discovery, death) is in this story, his very first, which few people have read and no one likely remembers.

Binyavanga was notoriously careless about his archive. And yet it puzzled me that he would let something as fresh and wonderful as this stay buried for so long. Now, I think, perhaps it was deliberate. Perhaps he did not want anyone to see this fully formed story about his fully formed self, written at the tender age of twenty-five, with all the heartbreaking honesty and acuity of youth, until he was ready—until his own helium-ballooned mind made its final ascent, pushing at the edge of the stratosphere with nowhere left to go.

Two goldfish were arguing in their bowl,
"If there is no God, who changes our water every week?"

Allotropy: property of certain elements to exist
in two or more distinct forms.

CHAPTER ONE

Dawn, December 27th, 1999 . . .

Jango had often pictured his imagination as a helium-filled balloon, rather than one containing air. As he rose above the wreckage of the car, a whole-body feeling came over him. His life had ended, the string was cut, and his imagination was free to merge with reality. He felt immensely liberated—like he was flexing muscles that had not been used in a long time.

Oh, to stretch! His body felt loose-limbed and weightless and his mind poised to soar. How could he have stayed in cramped earthliness for so long? How could he have forgotten this feeling? Had he not once danced with stars and had dalliances with gods?

Was he dreaming? Or was this part of some spectral past life? He felt no trauma of the type normally associated with violent death. Right now, he was rather piqued that he had missed out on the nonstop partying that was taking place all over the World. He hugged himself and found that his body seemed intact. He found it odd that he did not seem to feel the trepidation he would have expected if there was a possibility that he was destined for Pastor Vimba's "LAKE OF FIYYRRE!" that starred a leering Red Devil and promised "EEETERNALL DAMNATIONNN!" He giggled at the thought. "Tsk, tsk, Jango," he said to himself. "You're getting above yourself!"

Oddly enough, right now the thought of going to "Heaven" and spending eternity dressed in white robes, blissfully ensconced behind Pearly Gates while drinking nectar or listening to harps was depressing. After spending most of his life in Johannesburg, and especially after the hedonism of the past few days, the "fires of hell" acquired a certain appeal.

There was another possible destination, though. His father's mania. To become an esteemed ancestor, as Zulu tradition dictated. Yet he could not visualize himself tolerating eternity as an "Outraged Ancestor," imposing droughts and plagues on disobedient descendants and anybody else who happened to be in the vicinity. Ancestor worship was a religion his father had tried to drum (quite often literally) into his head, and it was one he had discarded with relief. The concept of ancestors scrutinizing and guiding peoples' lives had always inspired images of power-mad old voyeurs playing African roulette (giggle, giggle . . . whom shall we play with next—Rwanda?)

What if one descended from a long line of arseholes?

He thought to himself that if he had a choice, he would not mind being dispatched to some sort of Spectral Cyberspace, if such a fanciful place could exist. Hmm, yes. Maybe he was on his way to a place where nobody would dictate to him how to live his life.

Oops.

Afterlife.

Pah! Banish the thought. There were probably harp-playing Censors lovingly denying souls/spirits or whatever their daily fix of Ambrosia if they did not conform.

As he floated with a sort of predetermined aimlessness, he delighted in his new rubber-bandy self, vaguely wondering why he seemed to have carried his body with him. Surely his real body was still getting intimate with the mangled metal of his car?

He looked down at the surrealistic African visage below him. It was as if Earth relinquished its pull on him. Relinquished all the trauma that he expected to have felt after the accident; relinquished all the weighty emotions and burdensome responsibilities that did not endear themselves to his new weightless self.

Or maybe he was still stoned from the party.

Around and below him, Earth had decided to stake its claim. A sudden gust of wind whipped itself up into a frenzy of anger, and lightning seared the ground. Thunder roared as if backing up the sky's claim on him. Massive, engorged clouds lay low and gave birth to reluctant raindrops.

This drama had no physical effect on him. It seemed that he was in a dimension beyond Earth now. He could not remain unmoved by her mourning, though. As the wind wailed in fury, he mimicked it, roaring his farewell to her.

Meanwhile, fast asleep at her home in Diepkloof, Soweto, Mama Jango moaned as the cloud of unformed premonition that floated past her house darkened her pedestrian dreams. A shadow of loss chilled her briefly. Later she would wonder, and trusty Pastor Vimba would come up with a satisfactory supernatural explanation.

Meanwhile, exultation welled in Jango as he looked below him and saw the grand panorama of the storm-enlivened city below him. A powerful love for what had been his adopted home for twenty-seven years overwhelmed him. Wordsworth's famous sonnet, a personal favorite, came to mind, and he laughed, stretching his arms wide and bellowing in exultation:

"Earth has not anything to show more fair. Dull would he be of soul who could pass by a sight so FUCKING touching in its majesty. This City now doth, like a garment, wear . . . "

Suddenly a force lifted the flat veldt and highways below him as if they were merely a tablecloth and swallowed them. In no time everything earthly below him, the mine dumps, squatter camps, towers, domes, theaters and temples of Johannesburg, disappeared the same way. Evaporated by something that seemed to have no substance or form.

Jango found himself surrounded by nothingness.

And all that mighty heart is lying still.

***

Stasis.

Silence so absolute, it screamed louder than anything he had ever experienced.

The sensation was terrifying. Utter nothingness surrounded him. There was no light, no darkness, nothing to feel or touch. Unearthly cold imprisoned his body. He began to shake and shudder, but soon even his shudders became sluggish and eventually ceased.

He was immobile.

In the absolute silence, he could not tell whether he was still floating. An excruciating numbness began to spread all over his body. Soon his body lost all feeling. He lowered his eyes to see what was happening and to his horror saw that something was eliminating it with a devastating silence.

As if it had never been there.

Finally, only the feeling that his mind was present remained, and it screamed into the nothingness to make itself heard. It tried all manner of activities to convince itself that it would be all right, but waves and waves of self-doubt assaulted it as it found nothing to compare or process. Nothing to perceive.

Not even an echo.

Shutdown began in some areas of his mind, and the rest reacted by exaggerating their most recent functions. Oh shit! This is it! He thought frantically to himself, this is how it ends. Huge, terribly distorted images thrust themselves to the forefront of his consciousness as it tried to resist the terrible finality of its surroundings. Now all that remained were the screams of tortured metal, flashing lights, his crazed screams, and the smell of feces and smoke. His mind accepted these gratefully as evidence that there was existence, that he did exist. These scenes played themselves over and over as the shutdown continued undeterred, becoming more and more scrambled and indecipherable as more functions shut down.

Then there was just nothing.

CHAPTER TWO

"Is it a kind of dream . . .
Following the river of death downstream"
— Art Garfunkel

Something enveloped him luxuriously.
Light, or a beginning of awareness?

Starting with his toes, he tingled with it, and it spread until every part of him glowed with its warmth. It was the strangest feeling, as if he had been recreated as light; his shape a memory of his earthly body. Nothingness still surrounded him, but he was now a spiritual glowworm, cocooned in what he could only think of as a life-fire. Every part of him took flame as his body memory emphatically affirmed and embraced his being. Tiny raptures exploded all over his mind; life thrills and memories concentrated into tiny capsules of pure feeling.

Again, his recent trauma seemed to have had no major effect on him. He did not want to try to understand it. He felt so good.

Children dressed in all manner of cultural pajamas floated past him, playing in their dreamscapes as if this place was home. Again, that feeling of acquaintance with this place struck him. This time he was sure that at some early part of his life he had straddled this place and Earth without conflict. Oh, to bathe in this light again!

He felt a fleeting sadness that these children would soon be tethered to life on Earth, as its chains embraced them with ever-increasing possessiveness. Don't wake me up mummy!

"Enjoy it while you can kids," he thought.

He looked above him and saw his naked body mirrored and magnified in a huge translucent gelatinous mass that covered the sky. Saw the long black limbs, the chunky muscle. The hated feet were stretched taut. Saw the face, a rictus of anticipation. Then his eyes trampolined the soft, large lips and clambered up the jutting mountains that were his cheekbones, scratching themselves against his toothbrush stubble on their way up.

Looking down from the summit, two large eye-pools below hypnotized his own. Irresistibly drawn to their twins, they dived off the cliff into themselves, and his soul swallowed them.

Light! Oozing out of the mirrored eyes. Light stained brown with their color lit the cloud, dazzling Jango with its brilliance. Oh, the ecstasy! It was his light! His essence! He could feel it coming alive in his body, burning its way up from his feet to neck, roller-coastering through the pathways of his mind, setting them alight with its force, then blazing out of his eyes to meet its reflection. They made contact, and the universe around him exploded.

He was somewhere else.

***

His eyes took time to adjust to the light. He was in a world that seemed to comprise nothing but living color. Dancing light was all around him. Heavenly shadows? Directly in front of him, a small tornado of light twisted itself and took on the shape of a person. Then it began to fade and assumed more human features.

An old man had materialized before him. An extremely sour-faced old man. His hair was waist long and in dreadlocks. He wore a three-piece suit, complete with bowler hat. Instead of a tie, there was what looked like a desiccated human ear at the end of a leather thong around his neck. The old man was squatting, African-fashion, and hovered three feet in the air fiddling with the ear as though it was some kind of talisman.

It was around this time that it occurred to Jango that this was no Heavenly Emissary. His helium balloon began to lose altitude.

Bleak, bitter eyes turned to face him.

"Ah, you're the newcomer," he began. "I presume my accent is comprehensible to you. I learned it in anticipation of your arrival. Let me see . . . Black, English-speaking, Dekaff, I believe you would call it . . . er . . . with a slight urban Zulu accent . . . car accident on the Johannesburg-Pretoria highway. Pity about the BMW . . . "

Jango did not find this dour-peeping Thabo amusing. Was that really a human ear? A white man's ear? Did they not have a Public Relations department here? This man was more bitter than malaria medication. Yup, no chance this was Heaven. Oh shit! This was either Hell or Rwandan Rouletteville.

"Hima Tata!" he burst out. "Where is this place, and who the . . . er . . . heaven are you? Is this some sort of celestial prank?"

Malaria-face adopted an even sourer expression—if that were possible. "I have often thought so. You are now in what we call African Binguni, part of the Otherworld. Souls here have complete freedom to explore just how mad they can be. You would not believe what perversions prowl in this place. I left Binguni in disgust. Nothing is sacred to these immoral Immortals. I am waiting to be transferred to African Presbyteria, you'll do well to do the same. Their harp band is famous all over the heavens!"

Jango shuddered. Any place this anally overburdened body-part collector did not like was probably his kind of Heaven. This African Binguni place sounded like fun.

A thin smile distorted the old man's features. "I understand you are one of the highlights at the Millennial Celebrations. They have chosen you for their insane new experiment. I do not envy you. Now enough chitchat, I will summon Mshale on the Supernet, and he will take you to the millennial festivities."

"Wait a second, who is Mshale, and what experiment?"

The Churl harrumphed, "He is one of your ancestors, a disreputable pervert even by standards here. Now shut up, they will explain all to you. My work in this hellhole is finished."

One of the floating cloud-like things turned into a large screen. With considerable surprise, Jango recognized what looked like a poached version of the Netscape Interfacer on the screen. The only real difference was that "Binguniscape" was written on the left-hand corner. Jango dazedly wondered what they did about copyright as he watched Kariuki reach out a hand and scribble on the screen:

HTTP://AFTERLIFE

And a website appeared on the screen:

WELCOME TO THE HEAVENLY WEB!
THIS MESSAGE IS SPONSORED BY "THE SUPPLIERS OF COMPUTER SOUL-STUFF TO BINGUNI"

Kariuki mumbled, "Can't be bothered to learn drumsong compuspeak," and wrote "AA.JangotoMshale@AncestralFair" on the screen. Jango was unable to express his astonishment as he suddenly found himself surrounded by darkness.

First to appear was a blue light that slowly formed itself into a banner reading:

WELCOME TO THE MILLENNIAL ANCESTRAL FAIR

Then the ground began to unravel itself: An unrolling carpet of hard, unrelenting African Earth, briefly tinted blue by the now fading light of the banner. Grassland, Acacia trees and scrub covered the ground. In the distance, Jango could see a feeding herd of Wildebeest and Zebra. A minuscule shaft of light appeared on the horizon, growing rapidly and becoming the sun. Its bright white light drowned the banner, then it turned red and sunset burned the ground and trees with its color. On the horizon the light shadows danced, numinous mirages of humanity.

From a distance Jango heard drums beating, and they grew louder, seeming to be coming from closer and closer. He stood still in fascination as this supernatural Cyberdrama unfolded.

As he dazedly wondered who designed this Supernatural Website, an enormous bellow interrupted the download, and it was followed by a string of curses in a combination of Zulu, English, and a series of languages that Jango didn't even know existed. Somewhere in the background he could hear music.

"HAYIBO!
THAT FUCKING KARIUKI'S DONE IT TO ME AGAIN!"

The voice sounded much closer now, and a body had begun to materialize next to Jango. The huge sweating figure that appeared in front of him could only have been the Notorious Mshale, his great-grandfather. Dressed like a cross between Elvis and a Hollywood version of "What an African Warrior Should Look Like," he wore a leopard-skin loincloth that had ridden up his thigh, leaving the head of a huge dangling penis clearly visible below the hem. A leather waistcoat studded with rhinestones barely covered his heavily muscled torso. His hair was dread-locked, pomaded, and piled on his head—sort of an Elvis becomes a Rastafari hairdo.

The man even wore blue suede shoes.

Mumbling to himself in Zulu, he tugged the hem of the loin-cloth down and rearranged his organ. "Damned Internet!" he boomed. "It really does pick its moments. One day soon I'll get revenge on that prig of a Gatekeeper!"

"Hello, Tat'omkulu, I am Jango."

Mshale laughed. "Do I look like a grandfather to you! Call me Mshale. I don't stand on ceremony. Sorry about my outfit—I was performing a striptease for some maidens from Arabian Binguni. I understand that you're another one who doesn't speak Zulu, eh? You don't know what you're missing, Buti. It is the sexiest language in Binguni. Yo! You should hear me doing Elvis in Zulu. The man himself has come to Binguni to see me perform!"

Jango, the free-thinking, "anything goes" liberal was beginning to feel a tad conservative and old-fashioned. What would his "the Ancestors are governing your morals" father have to say about this Rock-and-Roll-in-the-Hay ancestor?

"How did you die by the way?"

"I had attended a druggy new-age bash, one of those 'I love the whole world' millennial parties, and on the way home my car somewhat over-eagerly decided to hug a lamppost—at a hundred and fifty kilometers an hour . . . "

"And the rest is Ancestral, eh! Hayibo! You're lucky to have such a glamorous death! Would you believe the blasted flu killed me! Me! The great Induna, lover of all women! Come on, we don't have much time. I have a roomful of maidens baying for my presence. Let's get to the party!"

Jango's hand was grabbed by a huge, horny paw. Mshale mumbled something in Zulu and their surroundings disappeared.

Before any scenes appeared before Jango, the smell assaulted him, pungent and tropical, the smell of a marketplace or a marriage feast. Frenzy, sweat, musk, and sensual heat—the smell of abandon. The noise followed. It was loud and disorganized. He could hear laughter, conversation, and song, in a bewildering assortment of languages. It did not sound like anything Jango had ever encountered. It was as if he could hear every individual's input and everybody's drone all at once. The sheer intensity of it was unnerving, and his mind struggled to unscramble the confusion. Soon, amid the gibberish, he could hear snatches of sounds that his consciousness could make sense of.

"SALE! SALE! ENHANCE YOUR GLOW, SURF MY NEW SOULSITE FOR THE BARGAIN PRICE OF ONLY TWO HUMANITIES OF PAIN"

"SPECTRAL SEX . . .
CHECK OUT WHAT MY GENEMEMORY HAS COME UP WITH!"

Even a jingle?

"SOUL-SYTE DESIGNS . . . FOR A TRULY SPIRITUAL SITE-SOOUUL SYTE!!"

"SIGN UP FOR A COURSE IN THE NIGGAHS NEW DRUMSONG COMPUSPEAK . . . KEYBOARDS ARE PASSÉ!"

"MAMA SQUEEZA'S SOUL BREW . . .
AN UNEARTHLY HIGH"

"Going off to the soul clinic, I haven't been feeling ecstatic lately."

"THE 'PHECAL MATYRS' IN CONCERT! TAKE A TRIP ON THE DARK SIDE!"

"PUTTY & THE BLOWFISH: BODY MEMORY REPAIRS"

"JOIN THE CYBER-BER QUICKENING!
ACHIEVE NIRVANA!"

"EXPERIENCE PURE AGONY . . .
RECENT ARRIVALS FROM RWANDA!"

"TIRED OF JOY? TAKE PACKAGE TOUR TO BINGUNI DARK.
ECSTATIC AGONY!"

"DUMP SOME PAIN ON A DICTATOR HERE"

Before he had time to get his bearings, they were plunged into a maelstrom of humanity. What seemed to be a crossroad of souls, rushing in all directions, each hindering the other. Faces thrust themselves in his sight as he dumbly followed Mshale. Huge grins as if from convex and concave mirrors surrounded him, laughing, chanting, singing, arguing.

They were illuminated by revelation, faces overcome with amazement, eyes shining with enthusiasm, pupils dilated with joy, love, passion, and intensity. There seemed to be no logic to their appearance. Bodies danced with scant regard for anatomy or physics. A few passed right through him, leaving varied and intimate flavors of themselves in him. With every step, a swarm of locusts went wild in his insides.

The people who passed through his body seemed to infect it with their exuberance, and he found it hard to contain himself. A flood of hysterical laughter rose, threatening to engulf his control. He clenched his teeth and swallowed it down. It was promptly replaced by nausea. He much preferred that.

"Are you all right, Buti?" Jango nodded. "Keep yourself together, we're nearly there. The Welcome is usually more restrained, but we're celebrating, and we have been waiting long for you."

Finally, with Jango feeling rather like he had overdosed on something illegal, they arrived at the Millennial Fair, or maybe it had found them. Jango was not sure what was where, or if anything was anywhere. "This is a dream," he thought. "I have smoked too much pot, and I am tripping."

He did not need to pinch himself for Mshale's sledgehammer of a hand walloped his back and brought him to a stinging awareness of his surroundings.

"Welcome!" boomed Mshale. "What do you think of this mad-house, eh?"

***

What a madhouse it was. Unearthly chaos. And its sensory impact was devastating. He felt as if the world he was in was in constant motion, there was no foundation. His senses were being overwhelmed from every direction.

There was no time to absorb or digest the impact, and even if there were, he did not think that he would have made any logic of what was going on around him. It was as if people here expressed themselves with all senses through a multitude of media and dimensions. He could feel communication bypass his conscious mind and flow into his subconscious. Buttons rusty with disuse were pushed and doors opened to raw, virgin sections of his mind.

What was most terrifying was that for the first time he could recall the thin crust of logic, civilization, reason, and manners as not being in control. It had gone off to a far place and was helplessly observing the body it had served so loyally for twenty-seven years being taken over by pure primal sensation.

He laughed wildly, thinking, "Shit, now this is Multimedia!" The laugh turned into a growl, then exploded into an animal screech. His mind was wide open with all the filters gone, and its unprotected core was being singed by uncontrolled input.

From far away he heard Mshale's voice saying harshly, "Sorry, Buti, hold on for a bit, and I will seal you off from this." Amid the pandemonium that surrounded him, he glimpsed a flash of dreadlocks, and he felt Mshale's huge arms around his body. Then something that felt like cool water entered his over-heated consciousness and covered it. Relief! His mind attempted a brief resistance against this foreign invader, but a deep grav-elly voice crooned it to acquiescence. Finally, he felt himself completely surrounded by a pungent maleness. There was an almost sexual intimacy in the feeling that was disturbing. All his five senses could perceive Mshale completely. Coarse facial hair thrusting through skin and a shock of testosterone.

He remained quiescent, as his mind calmed down. Mshale's grip on it was solid and nothing penetrated. After a while, Mshale's grip relaxed, and his consciousness began to communicate softly with Jango's.

"This is my fault, Buti. We were so excited by your arrival, we forgot that you have not been formatted to face us all together." He chuckled, and Jango shuddered at the soothing vibration of it.

"You should feel complimented. It is not so often I soul-merge with a man."

He could feel the sinews of Mshale's body intertwine with his as they gripped his body powerfully, calming the violent shudders. He could hear vibrations, and it seemed that somebody was communicating with Mshale, a deeper, more resonant sentience, not as gravelly or harsh.

"Jango," throbbed Mshale. "I have spoken to Senkou. He is an old soul, the one who chose you for this mission. He will replace me as your mind's environment. He's better at this than I am."

That elicited a brief flutter of panic. "Relax," a murmur throbbed. "It will be seamless."

He could feel Mshale's essence seep out of him as another replaced him. Initially, it was difficult to discern the flavor of this person as it mingled with Mshale's pungency. Gradually, he had the sense of a deep, almost bottomless personality: it resonated with antiquity and calmness. In contrast to Mshale, he could feel little of this person's physical presence. Another difference was the bizarre sensation that certain essences of himself occurred in this person. This part of the foreign consciousness instantly entered Jango's consciousness and merged with its twin, giving him a feeling of peculiar comfort.

"I wish you peace and many raptures."

What a voice. Ripples as a pebble sank in deep waters.

Collection Missions-Etrangères.

Martyre du Bienheureux Augustin SCHAEFFLER, M. E. P.
décapité au Tonkin, le 1ᵉʳ Mai 1851.

93

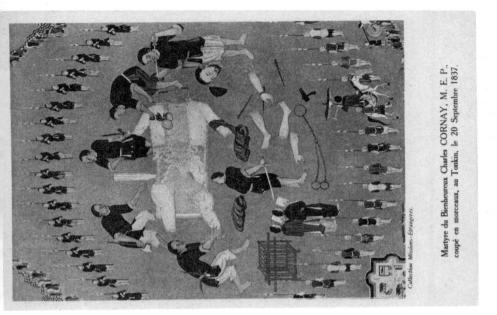

Collection Missions-Étrangères.

Martyre du Bienheureux Charles CORNAY, M. E. P., coupé en morceaux, au Tonkin, le 20 Septembre 1837.

POEM

Joy

Amatesiro Dore

Joy born into sorrow
Not by choice or the will of men
But the love in his heart made him gay
Fellow men said
Joy made God sad
Cos his love was male
Joy goes to hell
A room filled with hate
For brothers loving brothers
Shower him shame
Heaped with hate
Mangle his mind
His love is artificial
But enjoy his art
Songs of his heart
Source of his soul
Steal his soil
For he has no right to
Pass property to his partner
It must remain in the family
According to African traditions
Death for love, heart imprisoned
Honey was taboo, joy unapproved
A crime for two consenting adults
Or two similar minors
To love and be free

II

If God is love
Love is godly
If man loves men
Man is godly
Pastors of hate
Terrorists of joy
Poachers of love
Shooting happy men
Is love by force?
Can I love a God?
Who can't love my man?
And my love for men
Oh Benevolent Destroyer
Pillar of bearded prophets
Heavenly host of killers
Paradise is bed for bigots
Cornucopia of chauvinists
Christ returns for his take away
Men raptured into banquet of fire
I pray to remain here with my lover

III

My son loved a man and hate filled my heart
I love God and must kill them at first sight
I pray they change because I can never change
Not for love, not at the risk of death
Are you coming to church, my brother?
No love for the Lord! He broke my heart
His people hate my love and killed my man
Can't be with a God who wants me dead and
I don't wanna live in heaven without my man
Come my brother, God loves you still
You sound like God is doing favors
Love is not a favor, not to me, brother
I don't want to be tolerated or forgiven
I have done no wrong by loving a man
I just need more grace to love him more
Why should I commit suicide, bro!
Because a nigga loves a man
Because a nigga sucks like God
Because a nigga fucks like mad
Joy is a gift to pretty fellas, bro!
It makes you gay and happy
Are you gay during Ramadan?
Are you straight during Lent?
Cross and Crescent in love
My baby is a sweet date palm
We lay on the mat under the
Dogonyaro tree facing the West
His feet made me forget my faith
My meat made him accept our fate
Fourteen years to death, you and I
Forever living joy can't expire

READER

First published in English as the appendix in *Homoeroticism in the Biblical World: A Historical Perspective* (Minneapolis, MN: Fortress Press, 1998), 135–40.

Creation, Nature, and Gender Identity

Martti Nissinen

Homosexuality as a theological problem is, admittedly, a digression from the theme of this book. Nevertheless, it is relevant to reflect on two theological concepts that are used as hermeneutical keys in the biblical interpretation of same-sex interaction, namely, creation and love.

The authors of the biblical creation stories took heterosexuality for granted: "That is why a man leaves his father and mother and is united to his wife, and the two become one flesh" (Gen. 2:24). In constructing creation theology from the creation stories, one has to solve a number of problems that are not mentioned in these texts; the question of "homosexuality" is one of them. A customary perspective is that the creation stories express the original purpose of creation, which cannot be fully realized after Adam's fall, which caused the corruption of the whole creation. Different "unnatural" phenomena, things "against nature" like same-sex sexual interaction, are thus explained as a perversion that resulted from the fall.

To link "unnatural" with the corruption of creation, however, generates new problems. Notions of the unnatural or things against nature fuse together empirical observations, unconscious taboos, and popular beliefs about the natural sciences and laws of nature. Furthermore, it is risky to transgress time and culture boundaries with this concept, as has become obvious in the study of ancient sources.

There are several creation-related questions regarding sex and gender:

- What in human sexuality is created and what is not? For example, are human biology, anatomy, and inheritable traits created, and roles developed through social processes and their concrete influences outside of creation? In other words, is "sex" created but "gender" not?

- Is same-sex orientation created when it is proved to be genetic in origin and inherited, but not created if its origins are deemed to be psychosocial?

- Is the post-fall corruption to be seen as the cause of the difference in the lives and existence of homosexuals, transsexuals, or people otherwise different with respect to their gender identity? If so, are they responsible for their condition and, if not, for their behavior?

• What is the correlation between creation and gender roles? The traditional strict division between active and passive sexual roles is diminishing today in both heterosexual and homosexual relations. Should the changes in gender roles also be interpreted as a consequence of the post-fall corruption or, rather, as a sign of ongoing creation?

These questions will not be individually examined here; the aim of this appendix (text) is to examine the relevant grounds for answering each of them reasonably. To begin, the concept of "nature" needs to be defined. In modern language at least three intertwined meanings of this word can be identified: (1) the empirical meaning: the sum of observable facts; (2) the teleological meaning: the function and goal of natural phenomena; and (3) the cultural meaning: a synonym for the word "normal." These different meanings of the word "nature" appear both in everyday language as well as in creation theology and biblical interpretation.

1. In the first case, "nature" is understood as the whole of phenomena that can be observed empirically. In scientific discussion, there is a tendency to limit "nature" to this meaning, that is, to natural facts. The idea of "unnatural" or "against nature" actually does not belong to this definition at all, because, according to it, all empirically observed things belong to "nature." This concept is thus descriptive rather than normative. However, although deliberate manipulation of natural phenomena can be called "unnatural" or "against nature," values cannot be drawn from observable phenomena, and "nature" in a purely descriptive sense carries with it no moral obligation. Moral questions arise when nature is taken advantage of, when manipulating natural phenomena causes damage to humankind or the environment.

2. Understanding "nature" teleologically is linked with Aristotelian and Thomist notions of "nature" as an actual being with purpose and goal. This way "nature" can be also normative, because natural law orders the purpose and goal of each creature. The natural function of sex-

uality is seen in procreation. Thomas Aquinas, for example, divided sexual sins on this basis into those that are "against nature," like masturbation and homoeroticism, and those that are "natural," like adultery or prostitution. Even today the Catholic church considers all homosexual acts as "contrary to natural law" (Catholic Catechism § 2357) and thus speaks of "nature" in this normative sense.

A problem in this case is that the normative meaning of "nature" is argued from its empirical meaning. An empirical biological function is taken as a criterion for what is considered natural and moral. When it is said that "homosexuality is against nature because it does not lead to procreation," a moral norm is derived from a biological function, and values are argued from anatomy. But when a conscious decision not to procreate is accepted, not only for single people but also for those who are married (the accepted birth control methods), then the potential to procreate is taken as the moral criterion for proper sexual acts and the act is justified apart from the purpose of procreation. In this case the intention of the act (for instance, sexual pleasure) and its moral condition (potential to procreate) may be in conflict—and this is often the case in the actual sexual life of people in the West today.

3. The third meaning of "nature" is in many respects a popular derivation of the second meaning. In this, probably the most common meaning of the term in everyday language, "nature" equals common sense and the normal, "straight" condition of things, and requires no further argumentation, whereas things that are strange and different, disturb the order of things, and broken norms are considered "queer." Not everything of this kind is called "unnatural"— foreigners in Finland, for example, are not called "unnatural." Yet the Finns have prejudices and reactions against foreigners (especially those whose skin color or clothing differs from those of the majority) similar to such feelings against homosexuals. Common factors are cultural disturbance and suspicion of things that are "queer" compared with the majority. The criteria for difference are cultural and often based on unspoken agreements in society. They are also used to create a safe space against external phenomena that are felt to be suspicious or frightening.

The third, cultural meaning of "nature" is more abstract and less sophisticated than the first two. And yet it may be more significant, because cultural "nature" includes the prevalent values and norms and reflects their changes. "Nature" in this meaning is a societal concept, which includes the authority that regulates norms, the internalized taboos, and the inner solidarity of a society. It is not a matter of abstract phenomena but of concrete issues that involve everybody, such as the idea of "straight" and "queer," the sense of "otherness," the distinction between insiders and outsiders, and feelings of safety and insecurity.

These meanings of the term "nature" appear also in theological discourse of creation, orders of creation, and the corruption of creation. A problem here is that creation and "nature" are often confused and merged with social or naturalistic determinism.

Social determinism means that societal structures and roles follow permanent, strictly defined laws. When social determinism blends with cultural "nature," different conventions and taboos easily appear as "orders of creation." "Orders of creation," "the original purpose of creation," or "Christian anthropology" are then equated with the norms of a particular society and become instruments of power.

For instance, the subordination of women, societal discrimination, or the hierarchy of races have in different times and places been considered natural conditions based on the orders of creation and Christian anthropology. The people of sub-Saharan Africa found that they were "Negroes" only when white people intruded into their lands. The midwife for "orders of creation" that led to apartheid was colonialism, and its biblical justification was drawn from Genesis 9:18–26, in which Ham's descendants are cursed as slaves of others. Thus, a class was created that was defined from the European's perspective. The history of homosexuality follows the same route: a group of people, pathologized by European medicine and psychology, was marginalized in accordance with the alleged orders of creation and on a biblical basis.

To consider creation or nature as a static condition or a series of events according to absolute laws of nature would lead to naturalistic determinism. There is really no such single rule to which all phenomena and creatures could conform. To see "nature" as a machine in which each part serves its own function is reminiscent of the Enlightenment's mechanistic notion of "nature" and easily leads to rigid functionalist definitions. The determinist or functionalist models do not seem appropriate to creation theology; it is not right to denounce all departures from the ideal as the results of corruption that came with the fall. If creation is not a static condition but constantly rejuvenating, we can understand that it looks different in different times, in the material world as well as in social communities. A person's gender identity also is evidently variable and does not follow rigid laws. The emergence of people with gay and lesbian identities in this [past] century is an example of this. The fundamental question, then, is the basis from which the variation of a person's gender identity can or cannot be seen as an expression of continuing creation.

As a result of modern development, the question of nature and creation has come to center around sexual orientation and related behavior. This has happened at the expense of other factors of gender identity. The main question has been whether homosexuality is inborn or chosen, and how homosexual behavior might be justified, if at all. It is not only one's sexual orientation and the respective sexual practice that is at stake here, however, but also gender identification and roles. Creation theology cannot ignore gender roles, because people as created beings not only are men and women but also live as men and women in a gendered society. A further problem for creation theology rises when gender identification in some persons (that is, transsexuals) is evidently in contradiction with their anatomical sex: in other words, a person living in a woman's body feels himself a man, or vice versa. Creation theology thus touches on all the main problems regarding the interpretation of gender. Only a heterosexist bias could make homosexuality a separate issue and exclusively a sexual matter.

Sexual orientation is only one component of gender identity, and its significance varies from person to person. If a person's orientation does not coincide with general expectations, the role of such orientation in a person's identity becomes emphasized — because of society rather than the person himself or herself. This happens when homosexuality is externalized as an exception or curiosity. Homosexual orientation itself may gain a measure of acceptance if it comes to be believed that the person is not responsible for it. However, because there are no generally accepted roles and self-presentation models for homosexual orientation, homosexual people become stigmatized, and their sexual orientation becomes the central characteristic of their personality in the eyes of the heterosexually organized society. One component of gender identity is distinguished from the others and becomes overly significant. This may result in imbalance in a person's individual interpretation of the self, which is projected back to the environment in different unwanted ways. This, then, increases society's need to exclude and externalize — and a vicious circle is in effect.

People create sexual culture together and share the responsibility for it. If love is not the motivation in this situation, fear, unfortunately, can be, and it can easily dominate people's attitudes. In Christian communities, no one denies that love is the preferred and desired attitude toward other human beings. All agree that people must love one another, even if they do not approve of each other's lifestyle. In practice, however, application of the rule of love is problematic. The catchphrase "love the sinner, hate the sin" has had only meager results.

Love must not be confused with "tolerance," which also is considered an exemplary way to relate to "different" people. Tolerance can be a paternalistic attitude that maintains different processes and systems for externalization and marginalization. The one who tolerates is seen as above the other. The distance and difference between the self and the other remains, because the need to tolerate requires that there is something wrong with the other person. Love, on the other hand, means stepping into another person's shoes, carrying his or her load, suffering together (sympathein). Love is not about striving toward an objective good but about putting oneself at risk for another human being. Stepping in the other person's shoes, we can see ourselves in that person and love him or her. This means understanding the other person from his or her own point of view, even when the person's lifestyle or opinions appear strange or wrong.

People do not spontaneously love one another as themselves but need a special command for that. The command to love and its fulfillment is decisive for Christian morality. Specific moral commands and norms are born from the needs of the time and place; the fundamental thing is that love becomes real and influential in this process.

As mentioned above, love is also the central hermeneutical principle when applying biblical commands, advice, and ideals to the lives of people today. The New Testament emphatically asserts, in the mouths of both Jesus and Paul, that the entire law depends on the commandment of love, that love fulfills the whole Law, and that the one who loves has fulfilled the Law (Matt. 22:34–40; Rom. 13:8–10; Gal. 5:14).

This applies also to the passages in the Bible that refer to homoeroticism. Making love a priority in applying these texts in real life does not imply all-accepting "tolerance" or the altering of God's word. To give love priority in biblical interpretation means careful examination of both the Bible and the prevailing reality in which we live with neighbors of flesh and blood.

Love and its fulfillment is the central principle also in discussions about the societal status and civil rights of people of different gender identities: same-sex partnerships and their public recognition, for example. For love to become a reality, traditional paternalistic, externalizing attitudes must be changed. The question "why is this person's sexual orientation something other than purely heterosexual?" may still be relevant. But another question is far more important, a question posed to everybody: "Why is the other person's different gender identity a problem for me and my society?" This question forces us to look into the mirror, which is the first step—a necessary step—in loving the neighbor as oneself.

Collection Missions-Étrangères.
Martyre du Bienheureux Joseph MARCHAND. M. E. P.,
(supplice des Cent Plaies), le 30 Novembre 1835, en Cochinchine.

Collection *Missions-Etrangères*.

Martyre du Bienheureux Louis BONNARD, M. E. P., décapité au Tonkin, le 1er Mai 1852.
Ses funérailles présidées par Mgr RETORD.

ESSAY

A Queer We?

Linn Marie Tonstad

In human life, no one gets what they deserve. Life ends in death. In that regard, we're all in the same boat, together in our separation.

All having is loss. Yet, to move as a mortal body that knows it will die is to have life itself, and life abundant.

No one gets what they deserve, but everyone deserves better than what they get. No one gets what they deserve: the damage I have done to others, or connived at, is never quite brought home to my doorstep. To get what I deserve would destroy me if it were calculated according to guilt, fault, and debt. To get what we deserve would destroy the possibility of us, for we cannot survive that calculus. But to get more than we deserve might set us free: from desert, from the logic of merit, but also free for relations beyond calculation, for a justice outside the law of responsibility, consequence, and blame.

We work against unjust deaths, but where do we go to rage against death itself? A world without death is not something we can work for (for the denial of death is the denial of life), but nonetheless we long for more than this, for ourselves and for each other.

Even if a good death is the only ultimate bodily mercy, there are mercies that aren't ultimate: local mercies, moments of respite, an unexpected smile or fuck, a kindness. In a state of emergency, when do we get to ask what life is worth living, and what, beyond mere survival, we are living for? As Audre Lorde said, some of us were never meant to survive (from the poem "A Litany for Survival," 1978). And mere survival is not enough: we want more. When survival is all some of us are offered, and others of us not even that, it is time to demand more, much more—pressed down and running over.

In a time when life together means bodily life apart, a queer "we" must demand much more than this. To preserve the possibility of "we," we have had to distance ourselves from each other in the ways that matter most. But life apart is for the sake of life together; without life together, life apart is not life. Life apart shows us its impossibility, for life apart is unsustainable. The life to come must reflect what we are learning. Our need for each other remains, regardless of our desire, and our desire is for each other. Who will we become?

To be a queer "we" means not knowing who we are nor who we might become. We have thrown ourselves willingly, riskily, desperately into the space of possibility. We have discovered our desire, trusted it, and been overmastered by it.

A queer "we" should be a threat to civilization as we know it, or as we knew it. Since the formation of a "we" always inaugurates a "they," a queer "we" must be formed aslant. A queer "we" cannot come from sameness, inclusion, or recognition. A queer "we" takes shape against the systems that produce sameness, inclusion, and recognition as their only possible ideals.

So, who is for us, and who is against us? Queer, the identity, can always form a "we" by distinction and distance: "We are not like those queers over there. We are not a threat. We are good citizens who simply want to love our families, for love is love." But queer, the political position, cannot form a "we" in the same way. As a political position, a queer "we" forms around those who have had the choice made for them: the unassimilable. Queer, as a political position, stands with those who don't have the choice to conform or to belong, and not with those whose nonconformity can be turned on or off at will. As a political position, queer is not a romantic ideal of individual dissent but a finding oneself alongside others who never had the option to walk through the door of inclusion, respectability, and power.

To speak is to risk—to speak for "us" even more so—but all risks are not the same. Insurance companies are in the business of

quantifying risk; a queer "we" is not. It is diffi-
cult to hold these insights together, but to opt
for one over the other is an unsurvivable con-
cession to the demands of transparency, leg-
ibility, the calculable. A queer "we" refuses
the demands of respectability and productivity,
even though some queers want these same ide-
als. Therefore, a queer "we" is not inclusive; a
queer "we" knows that enmity and antagonism
are real.

A queer "we" reflects an ethics in which
antagonism is never overcome, even as we learn
that we are already in relations that destroy us
and remake us. A queer "we" knows that life to-
gether includes death and loss, that the body that
lives is the body that dies. And because death is
the necessary end, a queer "we" fights and grieves
and works for the life of the body that is so much
more than survival, so much more than living,
and going on.

Instead of reproducing what already
is, a queer "we" finds another option. As queer
theologian Marcella Althaus-Reid puts it,
"Queers are searching for God's nipples and soft
lips and trying to bite them in oblique ways in
order to achieve some oblique transcendence
in their lives" (*The Queer God*, 2003, 49). And
so, we become a queer "we," a "we" of strangers
and the estranged.

POEMS

BOP: RIGHTEOUSNESS

Chekwube Danladi

The Asr call to prayer sounds through while you and I
hotbox in your Honda Accord.
One of us, again, starts the pussy talk—how we love it,
when we learned to, recalling the nights we lay sleepless from
fear of it. Wouldn't granny call it Shaitan's steady progress?
How easily now we make ourselves from sin?

Cousin, let's not run away from fighting

the virtue we were given. Though I'd bet, at first,
on our certain dismissal from the property line:
should we be cast forever into the desert, recalling
our folks' lasting warnings *(Imagine your solitude;*
                          one child can kill its entire lineage,
                          so search for Allah's grace.)
together we can set our lips into a line, make pill the ill-will,
wash it down with shawarma and Radiohead.

Cousin, let's not run away. From fighting

Harmattan's dry ablution, its red earth biting
our eyes. Swipe at my ears and hands and mouth, taking it.
Repeat after me: cousin, we've been traumatized
yet still know how to love. So yes, we have won,
made the future have something to do with us, our
daring to sleep sound through the oblige of ancestry.

Cousin, let's not. Run away from fighting.

وَخَيْمة نَاطُورٍ برأسِ مُنيفَةٍ
إذا عارضَتْهَا الشمس فَاءت ظِلالُها
حَطَطْنا بها الأثقالَ قَلَّ هَجيرةٍ
تأَبَّتْ قليلاً ثمَّ جاءت بِمَذْقةٍ
كأنّا لديها بين عِطْفَيْ نعامةٍ
حَلَبْتُ لأصحابي بها دِرَّةَ الصَّبا
إذا ما أتتْ دون اللَّهاةِ من الفتى
فلما تَوقَّ اللَّيْلُ جُنْحًا من الدُّجَى
وعاطَيْتُ من أهْوى الحديثَ كما بدا
فغنَّى وقد وسَّدْتُ يُسْرايَ خدَّهُ
فأَنزلتُ حاجاتٍ بحقْوَى مُساعِدٍ
وأصبحْتُ ألْحى السَّكْرَ والسُكر محسنٌ
سأبْغي الغِنَى إما نديمَ خَليفَةٍ
بكلِّ فتىً لا يُسْتطارُ جِنانُه
لنَخْمُسَ مالَ اللهِ من كلِّ فاجرٍ
ألم تَرَ أنَّ المالَ عَوْنٌ على التقَى

تَهُمُّ يَدا مَنْ رامها بِزَليلِ
وإنْ واجهتْها آذنتْ بدُخُولِ
عَبُوريّة تُذْكَى بِغَيْرِ قَتيلِ
من الظِّلِّ في رثِّ الأباءِ ضَئيلِ
جفا زَوْرُها عن مَبْرَكٍ ومَقيلِ
بصفراءَ من ماءِ الكُرُومِ شَمُولِ
دعا همُّه من صدرِه برحيلِ
تصابَيْتُ واستَجْملتُ غيرَ جميلِ
وذَللْتُ صعْبًا كان غيرَ ذليلِ
ألا رُبّما طالبْتُ غيرَ مُنيلِ
وإن كان أدنى صاحبٍ ودخيلِ
ألا ربَّ إحسانٍ عَليك ثَقيلِ
يقومُ سواءً أوْ مُخيفَ سبيلِ
إذا نوّهَ الزَّحْفان باسم قَتيلِ
وذي بطْنةٍ للطَّيِّباتِ أكولِ
وليس جوادٌ مُعْدِمٌ كَبَخيلِ

From Philip F. Kennedy, *The Wine Song in Classical Arabic Poetry: Abu Nuwas and the Literary Tradition* (Oxford: Clarendon Press, 1997), 270–71.

Wa-Khaiymati Nāturin

Abu Nuwas

Many [is the] tent of a vine-guardian, on the summit of a high peak—
    the hands of those who climb up to fear slipping—
When the sun meets it sideways [in the morning] it casts a shadow and
    if it meets it face on [from above at noon]
    it invites [the people] to enter—
At [which] we have unloaded our baggage, put to rout by the heat of a
    dog-day kindled without a wick;
[The sun] tarried shortly, then provided a piece of shade
    [under a canopy of] shabby reeds;
[Thus were we] as if [snuggled] between the two flanks of an ostrich,
    whose breast is too rough to be the place for an afternoon nap;
There I milked the "best milk" of youthful passion for my friends,
    consisting of a white, chilled wine, the juice of the vines;
As soon as it is sipped by a young man his preoccupations sound a
    retreat from his heart;
And once night-time had taken over a portion of the darkness, I gave in
    to youthful passion, and found beauty and delight in ugly things;
I conversed with my loved one, without affectation, and humiliated a
    recalcitrant boy who was not shameless
    [by nature];
He sang [enticingly], whilst my right arm was a pillow to his cheek,
    "How so often have I sought after that which is unobtainable!"
So I unloaded my desires between the two loins of a "helpful boy,"
    even though he was my closest friend and [honored] guest.
I woke in the morning to curse [my] drunkenness, though drunkenness
    had been "generous" to me—how often has "generosity" been a
    burden to you.
[So] I will search for wealth, either as the companion of the Caliph who
    stands [as] an equal, or as the terror of a country road.
With any young man whose heart does not flutter when two armies
    call out in the name of someone killed:
Let us take God's fifth [of the spoil] from every reprobate, who has a
    paunch and eats gluttonously the goods
    [of the Earth];
Do you not see that the money [I collect in this way] thus aids my
    piety, and that a "generous man" left penniless is no [longer]
    a miserly [pious hypocrite]!

AGAINST

NATURE

Republished texts that have informed the foundations of this project. We acknowledge that debates on the notion of "nature" impact jurisprudence and theory can become a tool for advocacy.

READER

From chapter one in *Against Nature* (Cambridge, MA: MIT Press, 2019), 1–6. First published in the series De Natura, edited by Frank Fehrenbach, Matthes & Seitz Berlin, 2018.

The Problem: How Does "Is" Become "Ought"?

Lorraine Daston

In his *Anthropology from a Pragmatic Point of View* (1798), Immanuel Kant remarked: "It is noteworthy that we can think of no other suitable form for a rational being than that of a human being. Every other form would represent, at most, a symbol of a certain quality of the human being—as the serpent, for example, is an image of evil cunning—but not the rational being himself. Therefore we populate all other planets in our imagination with nothing but human forms, although it is probable that they may be formed very differently, given the diversity of the soil that supports and nourishes them, and the different elements of which they are composed."[1] The many depictions of the serpent with a human head who corrupted Adam and Eve implicitly make Kant's point: a serpent who could speak and reason so beguilingly was as much person as reptile. Although Kant was firmly convinced of the existence and physical diversity of nonhuman rational beings, he assumed that this diversity made no difference to their character as rational beings: whether they were rational Martians or rational angels, reason was reason everywhere in the universe.[2] I would like to offer an alternative to this brand of Kantian philosophical anthropology: it matters to reason—not just to sensibility and psychology—what kind of species we are. The kind of philosophical anthropology I am proposing is an inquiry into human reason, rather than universal Reason tout court.

  This project makes sense only when anchored in a genuine problem, one of sufficient historical and cultural generality to be a plausible candidate for a philosophical anthropology (as opposed to a cultural anthropology or a history of a particular time and place). The question I would like to address can be simply posed: Why do human beings, in many different cultures and epochs, pervasively and persistently, look to nature as a source of norms for human conduct? Why should nature be made to serve as a gigantic echo chamber for the moral orders that humans make? It seems superfluous to duplicate one order with another, and highly dubious to derive the legitimacy of the human order from its alleged original in nature. Yet in ancient

India and in ancient Greece, in medieval France and Enlightenment America, in the latest controversy over homosexual marriage or genetically modified organisms, people have linked the natural and moral orders — and disorders. The stately rounds of the stars modeled the good life for Stoic sages; the rights of man were underwritten by the laws of nature in revolutionary France and in the newborn United States; recent avalanches in the Swiss Alps or hurricanes in the United States prompt headlines about "The Revenge of Nature." Nature has been invoked to emancipate, as the guarantor of human equality, and to enslave, as the foundation of racism. Nature's authority has been enlisted by reactionaries and by revolutionaries, by the devout and secular alike. In various and dispersed traditions, nature has been upheld as the pattern of all values: the Good, the True, and the Beautiful.[3]

For centuries, philosophers have insisted that there are no values in nature. Nature simply is; it takes a human act of imposition or projection to transmute that "is" into an "ought." On this view, we can draw no legitimate inference from how things happen to be to how things should be, from the facts of the natural order to the values of the moral order. To try to draw such inferences is to commit what has come to be called the "naturalistic fallacy"[4] — a kind of covert smuggling operation in which cultural values are transferred to nature, and nature's authority is then called upon to buttress those very same values. Friedrich Engels described this strategy in his critique of Social Darwinism, which he claimed was simply a reimportation back into the social realm[5] of the Malthusian doctrines that Darwin had originally exported into the natural realm. Engels's example shows that this sort of value-trafficking often has political consequences, as when medieval rulers defended the subordination of a bulk of the population to the aristocracy and clergy on the grounds that it was as natural as for the hands and feet to serve the head and heart of the "body politic," or when early twentieth-century opponents of higher education for women argued that the natural vocation of all women was to be wives and mothers. Subordination and domesticity were thereby "naturalized": in such cases, contingent (and controversial) social arrangements were shored up by the necessity and/or desirability of allegedly natural arrangements. With examples like these in mind, some critics of alleged moral echoes of natural orders, such as the nineteenth-century British philosopher John Stuart Mill, have condemned the naturalistic fallacy as not just logically false but morally pernicious to boot: "Either it is right that we should kill because nature kills; torture because nature tortures; ruin and devastate because nature does the like; or we ought not to consider at all what nature does, but do what it is good to do."[6]

Why, then, does the moral resonance of nature persist so stubbornly? Critical thinkers have spilled oceans of ink in attempts to pry "is" and "ought" apart. Despite their best efforts, however, the temptation to extract norms from nature seems to be enduring and irresistible. The very word "norm" epitomizes the mingling of the descriptive and prescriptive: it means both what usually happens and what should happen; "Normally, the cranes migrate before the first snow." I am under no illusion that another attempt to put "is" and "ought" asunder will succeed where the likes of Hume, Kant, Mill, and many other luminaries have failed. Rather, I want to understand why they have failed: why, in the teeth of such sterling counsel to the contrary, do we continue to seek values in nature?

I do not think the answer to this question lies just in an account of popular error, vestigial religious beliefs, or sloppy habits of thought. This is a case not of simple mass irrationality but rather of a very human form of rationality—and hence the subject of a philosophical anthropology. My line of inquiry will be to excavate the sources of the intuitions that propel the search for values in nature. In various times and places, these intuitions have expressed themselves in the most luxuriantly diverse forms—as diverse as the efflorescence of nature and culture themselves. But the core intuitions underlying all this diversity of norms grounded in natures have something in common. At their heart is the perception of order—as fact and as ideal.

Some examples of the different ways natural and moral orders have been intertwined will help make the problem vivid. Because nature is so rich in orders, the analogy between natural and human orders can take many forms. Over the millennia, the authority of nature has been enlisted in support of many causes: to justify and to condemn slavery, to praise breastfeeding and to blame masturbation, to elevate the aesthetic of the sublime over the beautiful, and to undergird ethics by appeal to instinct or evolution. It would take many volumes (yet to be written) to do justice to this long and motley history and just as many volumes to describe the diverse natural orders used to represent and often legitimate these diverse norms. But certain forms of order recur over and over again, from Greco-Roman antiquity to yesterday's newspaper. At least within the Western intellectual tradition (the only one I am even partially qualified to write about), three in particular have exerted strong and lasting influence on both learned reflections and popular intuitions: specific natures, local natures, and universal natural laws.

NOTES

[1]
Immanuel Kant, *Anthropology from a Pragmatic Point of View* (1798), trans. and ed. Robert B. Louden (Cambridge: Cambridge University Press, 2006), I.30, 65.

[2]
Kant once wrote (in the context of how to weigh the strength of belief by probabilities) that he would be willing to bet all he had on the existence of life on other planets: "I should be willing to stake my all on the contention—were it possible by means of any experience to settle the question—that at least one of the planets we see is inhabited. Hence I say that it is not merely opinion, but a strong belief, on the correctness of which I should be prepared to run great risks, that other worlds are inhabited." Immanuel Kant, *Critique of Pure Reason*, trans. Norman Kemp Smith (New York: St. Martin's Press, 1965), A825/B823, 648.

[3]
For examples, see William Cronon, ed., *Uncommon Ground: Rethinking the Human Place in Nature* (New York: Norton, 1996); Mikulás Teich, Roy Porter, and Bo Gustafsson, eds., *Nature and Society in Historical Context* (Cambridge: Cambridge University Press, 1997); Lorraine Daston and Fernando Vidal, eds., *The Moral Authority of Nature* (Chicago: University of Chicago Press, 2004); and the still fundamental Clarence J. Glacken, *Traces on the Rhodian Shore: Nature and Culture in Western Thought from Ancient Times to the End of the Eighteenth Century* (Berkeley: University of California Press, 1967).

[4]
The British philosopher G. E. Moore first coined this term in the context of ethics: G. E. Moore, *Principia Ethica* (1903; repr., Cambridge: Cambridge University Press, 1976), 37–58. Since then, the term's range of references has expanded to include any appeal to nature as a standard for human values, see Lorraine Daston, "The Naturalistic Fallacy Is Modern," *Isis* 105 (2014): 579–87.

[5]
Friedrich Engels to Pjotr Lawrowitsch Lawrow, November 12–17, 1875, in Karl Marx and Friedrich Engels, *Werke* (Berlin: Dietz, 1966), 34:170.

[6]
John Stuart Mill, "Nature," in *Three Essays on Religion* (1874) in Mill, *Essays on Ethics, Religion and Society*, ed. J. M. Robson (London: Routledge, 1996), 386.

ENDNOTE

The Past and Present of Against Nature Laws

Living in a society based on a secular legal system with a religious imprint, we are subject to the concept and figure of "nature." It is used to criminalize individuals for nonreproductive sexual orientations, gender identities, and ways of being. This affects primarily LGBTQI+ communities, but it extends beyond them too. The legal language to support such criminalization often stems from colonial legal codes: the Napoleonic Penal Code, for example, and various other British texts. Defined in some Penal Codes as an "act against nature" (Article 534, Lebanon, 1943), "carnal intercourse against the order of nature" (Section 377, India, 1860, repealed in 2018), or "carnal knowledge against the order of Nature" (Article 162, Kenya, 1930), these laws often found no cultural base when first introduced to former European colonies. Using arbitrary concepts to divide what is "natural" from what is "unnatural," politicians, judges, and religious figures have ascribed an indisputable authority to nature (and still do), and such divisions are enforced with the full coercive power of the state. Over the past couple of years we have witnessed important legal changes however, especially in India and Botswana, which undermine this concept of nature; these are moments of hope, but more importantly they are occasions to discuss further developments.

Ultimately, challenging the colonial origins of the contra naturam laws is important work to do, and yet this work still remains insufficient; we bear responsibility for the continuing exercise of these laws and their related imaginaries. From north to south, the laws against nature have become a horizon for the politics of many conservative movements, who look for more control and uniformization of people's gender, sexuality, and privacy. This is also affecting countries that were once considered to be progressive, but are now witnessing a rise of anti-gender ideologies, the justification of verbal and physical discrimination toward trans individuals, worsening environments for LGBTQI+ organizations, divergent legal statuses and reproductive rights for LGBTQI+ families, as well as the threat to abortion rights for women.

To monitor current state jurisdictions, charts, maps, and rankings are produced by international NGOs, like the International Lesbian, Gay, Bisexual, Trans and Intersex Association (ILGA). Beyond criminalization their research also takes into account instances of expression, freedom of association, protection (constitutional, individual, professional), and the recognition of marriage, partnership, and adoption. This map, inverted and visually translated, is offered here as a tool to visualize the work that still needs to be done.

Discrimination is not only enforced by the state, and while international advocacy is more necessary than ever, human dignity and equality enacted on a personal level must become part of rethinking the social and legal imaginary, to which *The Against Nature Journal* hopes to contribute.

Grégory Castéra and Giulia Tognon
Editors

MAP

The data presented in this map is based on "State-Sponsored Homophobia," an International Lesbian, Gay, Bisexual, Trans and Intersex Association (ILGA) report by Lucas Ramón Mendos, December 2019. Courtesy of ILGA World. Map drawn by Stepan Lipatov.

CALEM

Marseille, France

is an organization founded by Imam Ludovic-Mohamed Zahed, the founder of the first European inclusive mosque in Paris. CALEM offers advice and training to a variety of organizations on topics such as migration, women's rights, and progressive Islamic theology.

calem.eu

House for All Sinners and Saints

Denver, Colorado

is a congregation of the Evangelical Lutheran Church in America started by pastor Nadia Bolz-Weber. It describes itself as "a group of folks figuring out how to be a liturgical, Christo-centric, social justice oriented, queer inclusive, incarnational, contemplative, irreverent, ancient-future church with a progressive but deeply rooted theological imagination."

houseforall.org

Reformation Project

Dallas, Texas

is a Bible-based, Christian organization founded by Matthew Vines. It works to promote inclusion of LGBTQ people by reforming church teaching on sexual orientation and gender identity.

reformationproject.org

The Institute for Art, Religion and Social Justice

New York City

was founded in the spring of 2009 under the leadership of artist AA Bronson and Kathryn Reklis. The Institute's mission is to explore the relationship between art and religion through the lens of social justice.

artreligionandsocialjustice.org

House of Rainbow

Lagos, Nigeria

fosters relationships among Black, Asian, Minority Ethnic (BAME), LGBTIQ+ individuals, people of faith, and allies in order to create a safer and more inclusive community. Reverend Jide Macauly is the founding Pastor of House of Rainbow.

houseofrainbow.org

Union Theological Seminary

New York City

is an independent, ecumenical seminary with a commitment to interreligious engagement. Progressive theology has long taken shape at Union, where faith and scholarship meet to reimagine the work of justice.

utsnyc.edu

ADVERTISEMENT

RAUPE-NIMMERSATISM by SAVVY Contemporary

Berlin —
September to November 2020

Raupenimmersattism. The Affluent Society As Consumed Society Or The Myth Of Endless Production and Consumption. A research, exhibition, discourse and performance project.

WITH Lhola Amira, ArTree Nepal (Hit Man Gurung), Yasmin Bassir, Mansour Ciss, Phil Collins, Sarah Entwistle, Samira Hodaei, Fallon Mayaniya, Daniela Medina Poch / Juan Pablo García Sossa, Jean David Nkot, Krishan Rajapakshe, Nasan Tur and more.

savvy-contemporary.com

MA in Transnational Queer Feminist Politics at SOAS

London —
from October 2020

The SOAS Centre for Gender Studies launches a new postgraduate program. It aims to refocus issues prioritised in Western Gender Studies and the study of sexuality on the complex specificities of Asia, Africa, and the Near and Middle East.

soas.ac.uk/genderstudies

Grupo Mexa in residence at Casa do Povo

Sao Paolo —
collaborating since 2016

GRUPO MEXA, is a group formed by people in vulnerable situations and members of the LGBTQI community. It uses artistic tactics to defend and promote encounters with diverse portions of the population in situations of social vulnerability.

casadopovo.org.br

On Riots, Grief and Parties at MACBA Study Centre

Barcelona —
until November 2020

How do dissident bodies survive in the city of Barcelona? How do desires and emotions fit into their displacements? How does the colonial regime continue to operate in these bodies and what wounds does it continue to open?

macba.cat

Desperate Living C-19 by Studio Voltaire

London —
June to October 2020

An LGBTQ+ artist-led program in response to COVID-19, providing support for artists as well as opportunities for people to engage with arts and culture in direct response to their experiences.

studiovoltaire. org

nominal bliss

online publication

nominal bliss is part of an ongoing series of free online publications that aims to develop new research networks around contemporary artists of non-binary and trans experience. The series is designed by Studio Vanessa Ban and edited by Wong Bing Hao.

Google nominal bliss or use this link:
online.pubhtml5.com/zkna/mhpb/

Interested in advertising?

Please contact us at:
advertising@againstnaturejournal.com

Tom of Finland Foundation and The Community

Paris —
2021

A group exhibition from the Tom of Finland Foundation's collection and a series of programming co-curated by The Community in Paris. The Tom of Finland Foundation in Los Angeles has been building and preserving the world's largest collection of gay and erotic art, consisting of thousands of works, since 1984.

thecommunity.io
tomoffinland.org

Contemporary And (C&) + C& América Latina (C&AL)

is an art magazine for the reflection on and linking together of ideas and discourse on contemporary visual art from Africa and the global diaspora. C&AL focuses on the important connections between Latin America, the Caribbean, and Africa.

contemporaryand.com
amlatina.contemporaryand.com

Iki Yos Piña Narváez & Jota Mombaça at Villa Vassilieff

Paris –
September to November 2020

As a duo, the artists will develop a research-based project focused on the delirium of El Dorado, rooted in the colonial thirst for extraction and on the inconsistencies of these white regimes.

villavassilieff.net

Collection Missions Étrangères.
Martyre du Bienheureux Pierre DUMOULIN-BORIE, M. E. P.,
décapité au Tonkin, le 24 Novembre 1838.

Danh Vo
Good Life
2007
b/w photographs

Danh Vo
Société des missons-etrangérés –
Les Martyrs
2009
postcards

Photographs taken in Vietnam, 1964–73, by Dr. Joseph M. Carrier, an American who worked in South Vietnam during the war years, first as a counterinsurgency specialist with the RAND Corporation and later on field research into the effects of Agent Orange. Although taken at the height of the conflict, there is little in these photographs to indicate the brutal ongoing fight beyond a series of bombings visible on the horizon of a scene of bathing youths. Instead they focus largely on young Vietnamese men, sometimes engaged in casual displays of affection such as holding hands in public or napping together. These interactions were accepted in Vietnamese culture as platonic expressions of masculinity, but Carrier's photographs are charged by a distinctly erotic gaze. For Vo, whose family left all their possessions behind when they fled Vietnam, including family photos, the appropriation of Carrier's images addresses a void in his own history. He has spoken of them as a mediated self-portrait wherein he identifies with both the photographer and the subjects.

Vo discovered these vintage postcards in the archives of the Missions étrangères de Paris, a Catholic organization that has been dedicated to missionary work abroad since the mid seventeenth century. They reproduce historical paintings depicting the violent martyrdom of French missionaries in Asia. Painted by Vietnamese converts to Christianity, such works portray local populations as ruthless savages in need of salvation and were used as recruitment tools for young priests. While a number illustrate their subjects using a flat, frontal style, others introduce techniques of compositional perspective associated with a Western tradition.

Danh Vo

is an artist born in Vietnam. Vo's projects emerge via objects and images that have accrued meaning in the world, whether through their former ownership, their proximity to specific events, or their currency as universal icons. Power, history, eroticism, personal biography, imperial dissolution and globalist expansion are all in play. The Vo family escaped Vietnam to Denmark in 1979, and the artist's work embodies the shifting and precarious nature of contemporary life. Vo imagines a world for the artist unbound by obligations to state institutions, social norms and grand humanist projects.

Thanks

Juho Aalto
Lawrence Abu Hamdan
Vanessa Agard-Jones
Marwa Arsanios
Pablo Bedoya
Francesca Bertolotti-Bailey
Pauline Boudry
Buenos Tiempos, Int.
Paul Dillane
EBC Publishing Pvt. Ltd.
Marie-Nour Echaimé
Every Ocean Hughes
Ambra Fabi
Joscelyn Gardner
Nayla Geagea
Hannah Gillow-Kloster
Natasha Ginwala
Eric Gitari
Abhijan Gupta
Alok Gupta
Juha Huuskonen
Aapurv Jain
Jason Jones
Tarun Khaitan
Navine Khan-Dossos
Adrian Lahoud
Renate Lorenz
Youmna Makhlouf
Carlos Motta
Sasha Moujaes
Suneela Mubayi
Siddharth Narrain
Émilie Notéris
Peter Nynäs
Emily Pethick
Gaëlle Porte
Achal Prabhala
Abdullah Qureshi
Theodor Ringborg
Bente Scheller
Gabriëlle Schleijpen
Ashkan Sepahvand
Mulki Al-Sharmani
Christine Tohme
Michael Toledano
Zeb Tortorici
Natalia Valencia
Marina Valle Noronha
Melissa Wainaina
Grant Watson
Kathryn Weir